Rise and Shine, Little Man

Rise and Shine, Little Man

David Hogarth

Rise and Shine, Little Man

Text copyright©2024 David Hogarth

ISBN 978-1-7393239-7-4

This book is a work of non -fiction. I have done my best to recall events and people as accurately and as kindly as possible. Apologies for any lapses of memory.

British Library Cataloguing in Publication Data.
A catalogue record for this book is available from the British Library.

1 3 5 4 2

 First Published in Great Britain
Hawkwood Books 2024
Blackpool Enterprise Centre FY4 1EW

Printed and bound in Great Britain by CPI Group (UK) Ltd.
Croydon CR0 4YY

For Mum, Dad and Kathryn

Always in my thoughts

mum and dad's wedding, 1953

CONTENTS

1. WHO DO YOU THINK YOU ARE KIDDING?

When I was a little lad, I kept asking my Mum and Dad where I came from. They said they got me at a stall on Fleetwood Market for sixpence. Abingdon Street market was much closer to our house, so I concluded that their story was nothing more than a comical ruse. Victoria Hospital seemed to be the most likely source of the transaction, and I was hastily returned there three months later to have some minor surgical alterations. The butchery I underwent was of a purely medical nature and not religious, if you get my drift?

Growing up, I quickly established myself within our family circle as the little chap who said ridiculous things. I was dubbed Bird Brain, or Birdy, and I assumed it was because of my love of birds. Sometimes at night, I would stand outside in the garden gazing up at the stars, wondering. I was wondering why I was locked out in the garden.

My entire existence has always been a bit of a mystery to me. I may never have been here at all if it wasn't for Hitler's love of my hometown, Blackpool. We were spared bombing during World War Two, because he loved to be beside the seaside when he wasn't busy doing his day job of being an angry psychotic murdering dictator.

I have had a very vivid imagination ever since my childhood. The next little passage gives you a glimpse into the sort of chaos that often resides between my ears on a regular basis. It will also prepare you well for what lies ahead.

Amsterdam, December 24th 1943. A young girl rides

her bicycle along a snowy canal path. She is wrapped up warm against the freezing cold. She pedals away whistling happy tunes she learnt as a little girl. Her heart is full of joy and excitement, knowing what it feels like to be young and free. She will live a long and wonderful life, and travel to many parts of the world. Earlier that day, she wrote in her diary, I long to ride my bike, whistle, look at the world, feel young, and know that I am free. Minutes after she made her diary entry, details began to emerge of a tragic accident involving Adolf Hitler.

Hitler is dead. Yes, dead. He ran over himself in a bizarre accident getting his car out of the drive. He was in a mad rush to get to an SS meeting, and things had just gone horribly wrong. It had been one of those mornings. He was running late, and his little Dictator alarm clock had failed to go off at ten past eight. Then Eva (his missus), had pulled her hero, and dreamboat of a lover, back under the Swastika motif duvet for a quick game of hide the Bratwurst. He was now a further two and a half minutes behind time, and to top it all off, Blondi (his Alsatian dog, not the 70s pop band) had chewed a great hole in his favourite little hat. "Nein! Nein! Nein! Blondi, und dumb strudelhumpf (I think that's right, I did French at school), you've ruined my favourite little hat, you stupid great hairy cretin. I'm late, and all you can do to help, is chew my hat into fritters." Blondi yawned, licked her lips, and looked at him for what he was… a complete and utter fruitcake.

"You could hang for this", the unhinged Fuhrer screamed, as he shook his fist at the bored dog's face. He snatched his second favourite hat off the stand, grabbed the keys for the Merc, and dashed out slamming the door behind him. He didn't even hear Eva shout, "Have a nice day darling. Drive safely."

Had he done so, he may not have ended up lying crushed beneath the wheels of his own vehicle. One of the gates at the end of the drive had blown shut as he got back into the car. Muttering to himself, and in a complete rage, he got out, and goose stepped back over to prop the gate back with a copy of 'Mein Kampf'. When he turned around, his big black Behemoth of a Mercedes 770 was heading straight for him. In a final moment of disbelieving trouser soiling clarity, he could have sworn that sitting behind the wheel, grinning from ear to ear in his favourite chewed hat, was Blondi.

"Gott in Himmel!" (What the Dickens!) The doomed Dictator declared, as the life crushing weight of his lovely car smashed the holy living daylights out of him. As he lay under the wheels, crushed, broken, and somewhat perplexed, he had his final thoughts.

"Blondi, my loyal old friend, how could you?" and, "My hat, my lovely little hat!"

He could see his second favourite hat lying a few feet away. It too, was crushed, broken, and no longer fit for purpose. The neighbours did all they could (nothing), and tried to lift the vehicle off him (not really), but it was hopeless. By the time the medics arrived it was too late, The Fuhrer was gone. The SS meeting wasn't the same without him, and after ten minutes of mickey taking at his expense, they called it a draw, surrendered unconditionally, and went for a few scoops down the Bier Keller.

World War Two was over. Blondi kept both of the hats that her master loved to wear, and continued chewing them to pieces. She didn't really miss him. He was an idiot. She enjoyed a long and happy life, and despite being questioned over his death, she was never charged. She wagged her tail and acted all excited when the Gestapo came calling, which threw them off a treat.

Like I said, vivid probably doesn't even begin to cover things.

However, rumour actually has it, that dear old Adolf actually planned to run a Swastika up the flagpole on our famous penis shaped tower here in Blackpool. Then he would declare the resort a playground for himself and his chums to enjoy at their leisure. Two big pricks for the price of one. That's why, before I told my tale, I thought I'd rewrite a bit of history. So there by the natural unfolding of history, go I. No bombing of Blackpool. My Mum and Dad get to meet, and a number of years later, a crackpot of a less murderous nature gets his chance to rise and shine.

Try as I might to have altered the past by thought or the written word, I cannot. How wonderful it would be (we think) to be able to do so. But, if God is in charge, then he chose defeat and suicide for Hitler. Somewhat poignant that he ended up doing his own dirty work. Time and the occurrence of actual events means that history is as it is. Or was. There are always consequences to actions, and there always will be. The future however, may be a little easier to influence and create. I hope so. Ironically, if we were able to change the past, I may have ended up not being here at all.

There is a sane and valid reason for the strange beginning to this story. I'm crackers. Well it sounds a lot grander than having mild mental health issues, or suffering from depression and anxiety. I think I had all three conditions after my Mum died in 2007. In fact, I was probably born anxious and depressed. I sure was three months later after running repairs back at Victoria hospital. Being a bit unhinged occasionally does tend to suggest a swinging door leading to somewhere strange and mysterious. Fast forward fifty odd years, and I'm still out in the garden trying to get back in. Sadly, both my parents are long gone, but I now have my own little home with no garden, and a key that opens the door to a life they provided me with.

Over the last few years I have felt something quite mysterious happening to me. It started after Mum passed away. At first I didn't really notice anything different, but I was aware that losing her had left a huge scar on my emotions and behaviour. I had suffered all the things that everyone feels when they lose a loved family member. Especially a parent. Boys and their Mums have a very special bond. I did with mine. She always tried to influence me to read more, believe, and have faith.

"In what?" I would ask.

"In good," she would reply.

Her favourite book was 'A Christmas Carol' by Charles Dickens. My Mum read a lot. Three or four books a week for most of her adult life. No wonder she was wise. Her many attempts to get me to read that book have always made me wonder why. It was its message and relevance that would provide me with something to use in difficult times ahead. The start of a thread that later became a lifeline. For someone who was beginning to sink to the bottom of the pond, I can honestly say, that my mystery, awakening, and enlightenment, only just turned up in the nick of time.

This is the story of the love between a son and his Mum. A young boy growing up in the sixties as part of a loving family unit and idyllic childhood. A family that may have never come to be, were it not for the fact that Hitler overlooked Blackpool during the war, and one of his snipers had a bit of an off day.

The off day I refer to was during my Dad's involvement in world war two. I remember him recalling to me on one occasion that he had been involved in a number of close shaves whilst driving his tank in France. It wasn't his own tank, it belonged to the British Army, but they said he could drive it as long as he was careful and didn't go too fast. His gunners had different orders. More along the lines of blow the enemy to pieces at every opportunity. They had stopped at one point to have a well-deserved break from slaughter and destruction on a biblical scale, and had parked up in a place they presumed was safe. As Dad happily brewed up on the back of the vehicle, there was a very distinctive fizz and a ping sound. It narrowly missed my old fella. Some sneaky adversary was perched in a nearby orchard trying to pick off tank drivers as squadrons passed through. Lucky old Dad I have to say. I have no idea what became of the chap in the apple tree, other than to say my Dad's turret gunner had words with him. It wasn't a long chat. God bless him, whoever he was. That was two chances Hitler passed up to prevent my existence. Thank goodness he never got a lucky third go.

2. STUPID BOY

My school days at primary, junior and secondary level were not a totally smooth passage from formative years to adulthood. I remember taking reports home hoping that my Mum and Dad would spot the one or two positive comments amongst the criticisms. Mum did point them out, but my Dad was less forgiving when it came to my chances of making it to a Grammar School. He didn't rant though. He was a gentle soul who had a fantastic dry wit. He tried to encourage me and warn me about the things I might regret later in life. But I wasn't the well behaved academic type destined for steady well paid employment for fifty years.

"Hogarth... you're an idiot."

"Thank you sir."

The teacher I replied to in this fashion shrugged his shoulders and sighed. *David seems to think he is the class clown. He should apply himself more seriously to his work and not be a disruptive influence on others.*

I wouldn't mind, but my Dad was pretty much the main culprit for my comedic approach to life. It was either Morecambe and Wise, Tommy Cooper, Laurel and Hardy, or any number of other great comedians that we would watch together and be in stitches over at home. I certainly wasn't the brightest bulb in the box, but I did fancy a crack at being the daftest.

Mum and Dad have both been gone for some time now, in the physical sense at least. There have been many occasions when I have sensed and felt their presence and influence around me. These little visits that they pay me are nearly always accompanied by strange signs that have become ever more difficult to ignore. To say that I was sceptical and cynical about that kind of stuff, would be a huge understatement. Mum regularly referred to me as, doubting Thomas.

"You don't believe in anything, do you David? Unless you've seen it with your own eyes?", and she would roll her eyes in despair at my complete lack of faith in just about everything.

"Have a little bit of faith for a change."

With regard to that rather large subject of faith, we were brought up Christian with a small c, if I can put it that way. Protestant Methodists, who would go to church most Sundays. I fancied some of the girls at Sunday school, so I didn't sulk if we were going on a Sunday morning. I don't think Mum realised this was my main motivation. It certainly wasn't bible class or the sermon that attracted me. Quite alarmingly, this fancying I had, did include somewhat older girls than me. The main reason my Dad wanted to go, was that he loved the sound of a church organ being played at full belt.

"Wait till Mr. Eastwood gives it big licks on his organ," he would say.

Dad wasn't someone you could have described as expressive emotionally, but he was always affected by the music he loved. He played piano, and later the organ. He taught himself to play by ear. By hand would have sounded much better I'm sure. He could hear a song on TV or the radio, and go straight into the lounge, switch on the Yamaha (it was an organ/motorbike hybrid) and bash out the tune in no time. I was brought up on Stephane Grappelli and Django Reinhardt. Most kids get milk and baby food. I had the opportunity to take piano lessons myself, but the fear of getting duffed up, and the fact that my piano teacher resembled Margaret Rutherford, meant I would only take a few lessons before packing in. Her perfume was so overwhelming that it caused temporary blindness and hallucinations for us both.

"You'll regret it when you're older." Dad insisted.

I was impatient as a child, no doubt about that. The fact I was unable to play Grieg's piano concerto with my eyes shut after three lessons, was reason enough to get back to kicking a ball around. I was like some precursor to a yet to be invented Bart Simpson. Always in bother for something and causing mischief. Fortunately I was minus his yellow spikey hair and skin. In actual fact, my hair at that time was almost identical in style to my Dad's. It was plastered down flat to his head with Brylcreem. It was neither Brill, nor cream. Parted up the middle, and then combed back to each side forming a distinctive point in the centre of his forehead. He had this one style for his entire life. Just like his own Dad did. When he got up in the morning, it was exactly the same, not a hair out of place. After he had retired quite early due to ill health, he used to sit around the house in a shirt and tie. Nothing else, just a shirt and tie. It was unheard of for his top button to be undone and no tie. He would be on holiday in ninety degrees of heat, swimming in the sea in a shirt and tie, with not a hair out of place. Okay he didn't go that far, but only because there was a sign that said, 'No swimming in shirts and ties... not even if you have immaculate hair'.

I had the equivalent junior hair styling substance, which stunk of paraffin, and was suspiciously pink in colour. My Mum did all she could to convince me that film stars of the day had this kind of hair style and look. I did point out that they were in their twenties and thirties, whereas I was only five. My protests fell on deaf ears. My Dad's swollen piano and organ playing ears.

For Dad, music always struck a chord and resonated with him. So much so, he would literally fill up and be so overwhelmed with emotion that he would be unable to speak. Even if I tried to break the spell with a quick funny remark, he was just somewhere else. I have inherited that trait without a doubt. A change of chords with some melodies and harmonies has the ability to produce that very affect in me. Play a tune that resonates with the Universe and it's amazing how the world responds. Don't be afraid to throw the odd bum note in every now and then. It usually brings a smile to someone's face.

My Mum loved music too. She was a huge fan of the big band sound, and in particular Glen Miller. On the day of her funeral I chose 'Moonlight Serenade' to be played at the end of the service. It was one of her favourite tunes. It reminded me of the times she and Dad would dance together at the Winter Gardens Ballroom. My sister Kate and I would watch from the balcony.

When that tune started to play, it dawned on me just how much I was going to miss my truly wonderful, loving caring Mum. By the end of the song I was in tears and felt unsteady on my feet as we walked out at the end of the service. It was the first time I had cried like that since the day she passed away. On that fateful Sunday morning, I had received a call from the nursing staff at Wesham Hospital, informing me that Margaret had passed away during the night. Despite thinking I was prepared for this, I was numb and felt really quite sick. I thanked them for calling and asked if it would be okay for me to go up and say goodbye. I wasn't sure if it was what I should do or not. Mum always said its best not to do that kind of thing.

Remember people as they were. I just really felt that I wanted to say goodbye. She had lain there for two weeks fighting to stay alive, and I had done my best to be with her when that final moment came. They had called me up a couple of times when it seemed the end was near. I would sit holding her hand for a couple of hours until the nurses would eventually suggest I go home again. They were quite shocked at just how much of a fighter she was. Watching her clinging to life like that was heartbreaking.

She was unconscious for three or four days and only having fluid through a drip. Alzheimer's had robbed her of speech and the ability to eat and swallow. A few days earlier the nurses had left a cup of orange coloured baby food and a spoon at her bedside. It was pretty much all she could manage to eat at this point.

I tried my best to encourage her to try it, as she wasn't really taking in much nourishment anymore. Because it was me, she sat up and I got her to take a couple of spoons full. It was hard work I could see, and it took a few difficult moments for her to get the disgusting looking stuff down. I readied another spoon full and asked, "More, Mum?" Her eyes said it all, she shook her head and said a very tired and weary, "No."

"Sure?" I quizzed her again.

"Positive" came the reply, with a knowing smile and a tone that was evidence she knew I was teasing. It was the last time we ever spoke, but for a few beautiful fleeting seconds, I was with my Mum again. Her last word to me, was 'Positive'. How very magical that seems to me now.

After the phone call I received the Sunday morning she passed away, I went straight up to the hospital. It was only a ten minute drive. I don't remember the journey there at all. Auto pilot along the M55 between Blackpool and the

Kirkham turn off. Then the closer I got to the hospital, the more I started to become emotional and anxious. The staff there had been really lovely in the two weeks my Mum was with them. The ward was very quiet, only three of the six beds were occupied with elderly ladies whose fate seemed similar to that of Mum's.

"Take as long as you like, David. She passed away in the early hours of this morning very peacefully. If you need anything we are just over at the nurse's station. Will you be okay?" the Ward Sister asked as she led me to the double doors into the ward.

"I think so thanks, and thank you for taking care of her so well."

She put a comforting arm around me and reassured me before walking away. I turned and looked through one of the two small windows in the doors. Although the curtain was pulled across at her bay, I could see the little pyramid of blankets her feet made at that end of the bed. It was over at the far side of the room, next to the window. The flowers I had brought a couple of days earlier were sitting in a large glass vase on the window ledge.

"You know you don't have to do this, don't you son?" her voice said.

"I know Mum, but I just had to say goodbye and see you one last time."

I had spent so many days watching her suffer, that I really needed to see her at peace. I walked in and down to the last bed on the left. It was quite hard to look really, but she just seemed to be fast asleep. Gone were the gasping and the constant bleeps from the machines. She was tucked up all cosy and her face was free from the struggle and confusion. I was okay for a few seconds, then I just started to cry. I sat down next to her, held her hand, and cried and cried. It was the most overwhelming sense of loss and sadness I have ever felt.

I was empty and lost. I kept whispering, "I don't know where you've gone Mum, you've gone, where have you gone?" Her voice was never far away.

"I'm here son, I'm here David, and I always will be here."

I think I must have sat there for half an hour or so until it felt like my emotions would finally let me stand up. I didn't want to. I didn't know how to go. How could I walk away from my Mum and never see her again?

"It's okay son, I'm okay, you know I'm always with you, and I always will be."

I planted a kiss on her forehead and whispered,

"I love you, Mum, I will miss you so much. Please watch over me."

At the end of the bed I turned back one last time, blew her a kiss and waved,

"Bye Mum."

It was even harder walking back over to those doors than it was coming through them.

Instead of leaving Mum there at Wesham Hospital though, in my mind, I had been to collect her, and bring her back home. She is here with me in my heart and soul, where she remains to this very day.

Over the following few weeks I felt very low. The worst day to get through had been the day of the funeral. The first day I remember any real kind of change, was when I went to the funeral directors to collect Mum's ashes. As usual, and without any encouragement from me, my mind was picturing me tripping up and watching in complete horror as the remains of my dearly departed Mum blew away like a wispy ghost up Onslow Road in

Layton. The urn was basic plastic and pale grey in colour. A label is stuck on the side to confirm you are taking the right collection of particles with you. After a brisk explanation of how to book an appointment to scatter the ashes at the Crematorium, I was on my way.

I had a grip so tight on this little container that I was almost crushing it as I walked back to my car. It is very weird carrying your de-constructed Mum around in a grey plastic tub. Once in the car I remember placing it gently on the passenger seat. I sat staring out of the window trying to imagine just how tragically comic this moment was. I couldn't. So I leant over and without hesitation I said,

"Right Mum, seatbelt on, I'm not having you tipping up and going all over the upholstery and carpets."

Next job was to get a slot to scatter the ashes on rose bed 25 at the garden of remembrance. This was not a moment I had looked forward to either. It seemed so very final and fraught with possible calamities of a slapstick nature.

Typically, I recalled a close to the edge joke regarding ashes that has always stuck in my mind. "What do you call the cremated ashes of humans?... Ready Brek for Cannibals." Hold on now, not so quick to judge here please! This was one my Dad showed me in a magazine, and we laughed with tears rolling down our cheeks for about ten minutes. I got my appointment booked, and Mum and I arrived at our allotted time ready to say goodbye one final time. An efficient and professionally pleasant lady took the ashes off me to re-house them in a special gizmo that allows slick and even release of your loved one at the squeeze of a handle. Should you ever be charged with this duty, do not, under any circumstances, squeeze the trigger prior to being at the desired drop zone. There may well be a trail of your parent or loved one stretching right back to the office if you do. In answer to your unspoken enquiry… no, I did not.

Standing at the edge of the rose bed, I realised that I was about to fertilise the soil and some beautiful white roses with the remains of my Mum.

I planned a figure of eight route in my head (like my Scalextric track Mum and Dad set up one Christmas), and had a few words with her before stepping onto the soil and squeezing the trigger. The ashes were coming out a little quicker than I had expected, so I had to speed up a touch to complete my circuit in time. They ran out just before I got back to my start point.

I breathed a sigh of relief that things had gone almost perfectly to plan. I gave the container a firm tap to make sure all the ashes were out. Well you don't want to arrive in heaven with a little bit missing do you!? I was pleased that my Mum and Dad were now back together again. Even if it was in de-constructed particle format. God willing, someone someday, will sprinkle me there with them. That would do me nicely, thank you very much.

After several more weeks had gone by, I had a very strong urge to go and buy an album that had been on my mind a lot since Mum passed away. It really did feel like I was meant to buy it for some reason. It was 'Long Road out of Eden' by the Eagles. I was drawn to a number of tracks straight away. They seemed so relevant. I was amazed and shocked at how the lyrics carried such relevance, pleasure and meaning.

After Mum had sold the family home some years earlier, and was living at her own flat, she would always insist on waving me off when I had been up to visit. It would entail her coming out to the communal hallway of the block, and waving and smiling through the window of the entrance door. I would always play heck with her, and tell her she needn't do this every time I came to see her. She would also pester me, and insist that I bring my washing up for her to do and iron. She loved to watch horse racing on telly while pressing my socks and undies. I watch the horse racing too when attempting to smarten up the look of my shirts.

During my late teenage years and early twenties, before I bought my own place and moved out of the family home, I would come home on weekend nights a bit worse for wear, and starving. To prevent me from drunkenly raiding the fridge at stupid o'clock in the morning, Mum would make a gigantic sandwich and a flask of tea and put it in my room. I never asked, but nine times out of ten, it was there.

Time to grab my bag of washing and get off home, I guess.

"Get yourself in Mum, you'll get cold standing there."

"Oh go on with you, it's only a minute, don't be daft."

One day as I was driving off and she was standing there smiling away and waving, I suddenly realised that there would come a time in the future when she wouldn't be there anymore. No more cheeky smiling face, no more loving waves as I drove off, no more Mum. I still own that flat, and whenever I drive away from it, I glance back at that empty window every time. It's just a window now. But I would give anything to see her standing there smiling and waving again. Anything.

3: HOME SWEET HOME

Which all brings me rather neatly, to a very key date. Well, key for me that is. June 2nd 1959. The day I said hello to the world, and thank you kindly for having me. Seven long years before footballing World Cup glory for our wonderful nation. A magical moment I would share with my Dad in our back room watching England play West Germany in the snow. Unusual for July I thought. I suspect our crank handle, twelve inch, two ton, black and white Telefusion picture box was the culprit. There appeared to be a whole lot more fusion than there was telly.

Apart from the very day I was born, I haven't spent a great deal of time in maternity wards. I am a childless sixty year old man who only likes well behaved children. They don't appear to make these anymore. But all kinds of children seem to like me. I can only assume that it's my high levels of stupidity that draws them to me. Like moths to a flame.

Actually, I don't think I've ever really grown up (thank God). As time goes by, we are pressured by life and society to cover up and hide away all the joys and behaviours we dearly loved as children. But that's our light, isn't it? The very essence of our being that connects us to the rest of the Universe. So much of being an adult appears to be an act, and everyone has the ability to act, even some actors.

"David! Will you please stop acting daft?"

Sorry Mum, no can do. My face in the photo in the garden with my Mum and sister having a good giggle, says it all.

When they brought me home from Fleetwood market,

our family unit was complete. Les, Peggy, Kathryn and yours truly, back to our cosy little three bed terraced home that would be filled with some very special memories over the next ten years.

It was filled with a great deal more than just happy memories of course. Mostly boxes of my toys. There were areas around the house for these to be stored so Mum wouldn't go breaking her neck every five minutes tripping over stuff. I did try to explain, that after the initial breakage of her neck, it would be highly unlikely there would be any further fractures due to paralysis from the first trauma. Pretty sure I received a clip around the ear for my impudence. It's a miracle I have any ears at all, as they were constantly being boxed and clipped like some out of control privet hedge.

The main bulk of my toy emporium was contained in two large cardboard boxes that had been pilfered from the local Spar shop. Mr. Gleeson, the owner, was most generous with huge amounts of empty cardboard containers he had no use for. They did the trick though, and stacked on top of each other under the stairs in the cloakroom cupboard was their own little home. I had a bit of a fear of the cloakroom for some reason. Possibly down to the dream I had where the door swung shut and locked me in. Then the light went out, and I could see through the cracks in the floorboards where a number of demonic creatures were milling around and preparing to break into the upper world to tear me limb from limb. Either that, or I just wasn't keen on enclosed dark spaces. The cloakroom was down at the end of the hallway on the right, and was often referred to as the glory hole. The entrance hall itself, had a small porch with a coloured tiled floor and a mat well. Oh yes, this was a small area that had been specially gouged out to be able to accommodate a roughly textured mat whose job it was to relieve your shoes of dog dirt as you entered the building. I was relieved more often than the other members of our family, which I'm sure doesn't come as a big surprise to you?

The front door was mostly a large frosted glazed panel, which meant guessing who had rung the bell and was standing there was great fun. On the inside of the panel was a swirly patterned iron trellis that made cleaning the glass murder, according to Mum. The inner door was three quarters timber with a glass panel at the top. This allowed you on tip toe, to take a peep and decide whether answering the door was justified. Milkman, window cleaner etc., had half a chance. Jehovah's witnesses and Police, no chance.

Once into the hallway you were greeted with carpet and wallpaper that would have frightened Zulus. This may well have been due to the overriding influence and final decision making of my Dad, who was a traditionalist and colour blind. Just inside the hallway to the right was a meter cupboard which provided further above ground access for the demonic cellar dwellers. I rarely, if ever, assisted with meter readings. On top of this cupboard was where our avocado and pea green two tone telephone proudly sat. It was to be used sparingly, and really only in emergencies according to Dad. Like if we were being overrun and slaughtered horribly by the creatures from below.

The hallway was a favourite venue for games of football between Dad and me. I usually got hammered, as he was in his late thirties, and I was five. I went in nets at the front door end of the hall. I got peppered with shots that I had very little chance of saving. I named myself 'The

Cat' after the wonderfully talented Blackpool first team goalkeeper of the era, Tony Waiters. A fantastic keeper who was tall, strong, agile, and a great catcher of crosses. Dad called me 'The Kitten' instead, just to wind me up. I showed him though, by bravely using my face to stop shots on a regular basis. Despite the severe swelling and bruising to my face, I could retire happy to my bed at night in the knowledge that I had only lost a hundred and sixteen – nil.

"Don't be silly David, you're at it again being daft. You used to love playing three and in down the hallway with your Dad."

"Oh hi Mum, yeah I know, I'm just trying to drum up a bit of sympathy here and entertain the crowds with tales of my unlikely hardship and brutal upbringing."

It was the same with cricket. Whether in the hallway, or in the back yard. Tie tucked in his shirt, and sleeves rolled up, it was like facing Freddie Truman at his peak. He came thundering in ball after ball. He even opened the back gate so he could start his run up in the back alley.

"David?"

"Alright alright, he bowled under arm at me for hours on end, getting me to either come forward or back to deliveries so I would have half a clue of how to bat when I went to secondary school."

I did cut loose every now and then, even after being repeatedly told not to wallop it for six as it could break windows, and we'd never get the ball back. I did give in to temptation on occasion, and mash it halfway up the back of the house opposite. This would be greeted with the furious double teapot pose from Dad, accompanied with,

"What have I told you about not thumping it for six, you nutter?"

Fortunately, I whacked it hard enough for it to bounce

back off the brickwork and back down into the alleyway. I usually got a couple of Freddie Truman type deliveries after that for my stupidity.

Down at the end of our narrow hallway was the door that led into the back living room. This was where most of our existence took place. The lounge to the front was only to be used for special occasions. Exorcisms, and watching 'The Val Doonican Show' on a Saturday evening, that kind of stuff. The living room was kitted out with a turquoise velour two seater couch and matching chair. A dark oak drop leaf table several centuries old that could seat about a hundred people, and a set of four matching dining room chairs. When the two leaves were opened on the table, there was no room for anything else, so we just peeped around the door from the hallway and wondered at its magnificence. There was a tile backed open hearth and fireplace with back boiler for hot water, protected, when lit, by a metal fire guard that I draped my frozen clothes on in winter before school. I smelled like an apprentice chimney sweep. When questioned by school governors, my parents refuted the accusation that they were using me as a brush to keep the chimney clean. I think my statement when I was quizzed may have influenced things. I panicked a bit and said I liked 'Sooty and Sweep'. I did like Soo too, such a polite and gracious young lady. What she saw in the other two barmpots is anyone's guess?

On the back wall of the living room was the statement piece of furniture that every modern family dreamed of owning. A sideboard. I think the statement it was trying to convey was, 'Aren't I hideous?' It was coffee and cream in colour with veneered sliding folding doors. When opened, it revealed a huge interior full of china and glassware that was never used, and a vast array of old magazines and photo albums. We regularly got the albums out to remind ourselves just how hysterical we all were when captured in photographic format. Me especially, as I was usually acting daft or facing the other way entirely. Probably because I was sulking at having my picture taken.

Under the sideboard was a gap that my football fitted into very nicely for storage. It was also a great hiding place for Judy, our Cocker Spaniel, when she had nicked a sock or some food from the kitchen. She would proceed to chew whatever she had pilfered into oblivion. All attempts to lure her out were greeted with ferocious growls and ear piercing barks to keep you at bay. My stroking her head flat when she was a puppy did seem to have caused some minor behavioural problems. I discovered though, that if I lay flat on the floor and blew raspberries at her, it was enough to enrage her so much, that she would emerge and attack me instead. We had many a tussle of this nature on the living room carpet. Rather than sink her teeth into me, she preferred to just slobber on me whilst growling until I gave in due to uncontrolled hysterical laughter.

I did actually use to play football in the living room too. I'm sure this drove Mum mad, as well as poor old Aunty Mary next door. I did develop a sound technique for keeping my shots low and accurate though. The constant thump against the skirting board must have been like Chinese water torture to anyone who could hear it. Most of our street probably? I must have been a lot smaller than most kids because our modest sized living room seemed massive to me. It took me ages to dribble from one end to the other and whack a shot into the corner under the sideboard. I did detour around the table and chairs quite a bit in a bid to make the whole effort more spectacular. My memory suggests, that between the ages of three and five,

I must have been about ten centimetres high.

I would stop playing indoor football sometimes, especially if Mum was making stuff in the kitchen. It was only small, with very few work surface areas. I remember being lifted up and sat on the counter top so I could watch her making cakes and biscuits, and preparing meat for steak and kidney pie. How she produced the food that she did out of such a small space is mind boggling. It was exceptional food, she could make anything, and it was always fantastically tasty. God bless you Mum. The best steak and kidney pie I have ever tasted. Short crust pastry made separate, and cut into chunks that would always get used up for seconds with tons more gravy poured all over them.

We had the usual array of amusing and geographically informative tea towels. They either displayed creatures acting daft, or a medley of uninteresting landmarks that you had long forgotten about. Mum always wore an apron in the kitchen to prevent getting flour all over her. This seemed to correspond with me being present. One of my favourite bits of kitchen equipment that I was allowed to touch, was the egg timer. A small clock with a twist dial face that rang a bell when time was up. Mum used to wind it up to maximum time, and the game was, could I stay completely still and silent until the bell went off. Because it was Mum, and the result would be delicious food at teatime, I played along more often than not. I pulled a variety of silly faces instead of speaking that kept her giggling, frowning and shaking her head.

Her head shaking was quite a frequent occurrence, as I regularly had to be rescued from bouts of my own stupidity. Top of the list was getting my tongue stuck in the whisk. I was simply trying to reduce the need to keep washing the damn thing, and relieve it of delicious raw cake mix. It was a whopper of a thing with double whisk turbines. I was forbidden to operate the gadget anywhere near foodstuffs that required agitating. I was allowed to play with it however, if it was clean and dry, and I promised to keep the business end well away from my mouth and partly mangled tongue. Mum had to crank the handle backwards on many occasions to release my face from the mechanism.

"How the hell have you managed to do this again David? You're not damn well right in the head at times young man, do you know that?"

"Solly Lum, hake hix is heelicious." I would try and explain, smiling through the blades of my tongue mangle.

When my face wasn't trapped in it, it made a fantastic double barrel machine gun for blasting Nazis to pieces. The handle to grip the whisk at the end was set at the opposite angle to the turning handle. If you held it tight into your stomach for extra stability, it allowed you to whisk like billy-o, and send a hail of fire and thunder out of the spinning nozzles the likes of which mankind had never seen before. I was relieved of my weapon of mass slaughter, with more frowning, head shaking, and the lame excuse that I was getting all hot and silly.

Hot and silly, was my default setting. To try and reduce my self-harm potential, Mum would sales pitch other items to me. There was the pastry brush, which had no injury likelihood at all, unless I tried to swallow it. I gagged, when the bristles sprang open and tickled the back of my throat.

"Give me that back, you idiot. What are you trying to do? Kill yourself?"

Next was the boiled egg slicer, which I foolishly mistook for, and played like, a harp. Mum finally stemmed the flow of blood from my lacerated finger tips with a bewildering array of bandages and tourniquets made from cut up tea towels.

"Just sit quietly at the table in the living room David will you? And read a book or something. I can't take my eyes off you for two seconds without you doing something daft." That long?

The tea towel first aid meant I couldn't pick up or turn the pages of any book. Not even my 'Rupert the Bear' annual, so I just contented myself by turning my wrists over very slowly and looking at pictures of boring landmarks and animals acting daft.

Anyway, back to the tour of the house. From the back door in the kitchen, there were steps down into an outhouse that was home to the washer and dryer, a clothes mangle, some cupboards for cleaning materials and a small coal shed. I did try to put my tongue in the clothes mangle yes, but I couldn't get my face close enough so just had a go with my hand instead. I have one very long flat hand, and one normal one.

The outhouse was a bit like a small conservatory, only with a concrete floor, and cupboards instead of comfy furniture to lounge on and look out through the windows onto the garden. So not really like a conservatory at all actually. It was more like my mad scientist lab, where I played with my little chemistry set, trying to create new elements that would change the world, or more likely, just the outhouse. I created nothing but mayhem, which usually ended up being poured down the grid as it was beginning to smoulder and crackle. Ah, the joys and endeavours of a young alchemist at work. How close I was to finding a cure for everything is anyone's guess. My own personal guess would be, not very close at all.

My other outhouse hobby had much more of a chance of creating something to wonder in awe at. Airfix model making was all the rage for kids at that time. The adverts showed, that by following the plans and instructions, beautiful aircraft could be constructed and painted to resemble the real thing. Many of my attempts would have spent their entire lives in the hangar, waiting for engineers to dismantle them to prevent loss of human life.

I was a little bit glue happy when trying to cobble together the grey plastic pieces. Jobs such as, fitting the pilot into his cockpit, attaching the undercarriage, and delicately fitting the propellers, usually ended up being forced into place and smothered in adhesive. I wasn't a patient child. All of this finely crafted hardware was now supposed to move freely to allow you to release your pilot, drop your undercarriage and have propellers that turned. None of this was possible thanks to my ham-fistedness and over exuberance with the gloriously smelly adhesive.

My model making adventures usually ended with me high as a kite having inhaled the addictive aroma until completely addled. Mum would usher me out into the back garden and help me fill my lungs with fresh air to bring me back down to earth. What the neighbours must have thought, God only knows? She would be slapping me on the back and cursing along the lines of,

"What are you doing David? What have I told you about sniffing the damn Bostik all the time?" This would be as I swerved and lurched around the back garden like a drunken fool singing 'The Bare Necessities' from 'The Jungle Book' at the top of my voice. I would imagine the neighbours were actually thinking,

"Oh look, there's that crackers little lad from next door off his cake on glue again." Something like that.

"I don't know how his Mum puts up with him, I really don't. He's as daft as a brush."

I did have entertainment value, that's for sure. Yes, some performances ended with the emergency services being called, but I'm afraid if you're making omelettes my friends, some eggs are going to get well and truly broken. I was only ever allowed to help make scrambled eggs. They were delicious except for the crunchy bits of shell. I was about as adept at handling eggs, as I was with Christmas tree decorations, which I also managed to crush to pieces. More of that later.

From the outhouse, there was another connecting door into the garage. This was a luxury in the early sixties, as many people couldn't afford a car. It smelt of fuel and paraffin in there. It had a work bench down the right hand side that had tin boxes and jam jars full of unused, and never to be used, nuts bolts nails and screws. There was a little vice on the bench too, and yes, I did tighten it up onto my nose and fingers occasionally. No other body parts though. I might be daft, but I'm not stupid. There was a window along the same side as the bench so Dad could keep an eye on me in the back garden. This was where I would be regularly acting stupid. At the alleyway end of our garden was a high back wall and wooden gate of the same height. The gate was painted green, and had bolt locks at the top and bottom. There was a further lever in the middle that slid across firmly into place when shut. I think Dad may have been expecting Hitler to pay us a visit some time. He would have struggled with the gate, but could have managed to climb over the wall I'm sure.

There were no broken shards of glass along the top of the wall to stop interlopers. People used that as a deterrent back then, and to stop cats wandering along the wall and pissing on your climbing plants. We had a regular unfriendly cat visitor who I had discouraged with my water pistol on a number of occasions. One day I decided to call a truce and lowered my weapon in a gesture of goodwill. I approached and extended my arm in friendship. It turned its back on me and sprayed me with urine. I later discovered the cat's name was Tiddles.

Back in the garage, Dad would be busy pretending to fix and mend things. He amassed a bewildering array of tools and bits of kit that he never actually used to any purposeful degree. In fairness, the saw did get used quite a bit, but that was usually to free me from something I had got entangled in. When anything actually required serious repair, he would call in his snooker playing pal from the church institute. Uncle Stan, as he was affectionately known. He was one of those loner type men who didn't really have time for women much. He was too busy reboring the engine on his motorbike, or making parts for his little canal boat cruiser. He was a lovely bloke, with a great sense of humour, and could repair or make anything. He had an inner kindness that often made me feel really sad that he didn't have a lovely wife to look after him. He was a bachelor, and lived with his sister and his rough coated collie dog Nel, who he loved dearly. She was always with him, even when he went off in summer to umpire local league cricket matches. He had a side-car for his bike that Nel would ride along in as passenger and companion.

Dad had a real admiration and affection for Stan. He was probably the closest thing to a mate that he had. Stan was as strong as an ox, and I can remember he always wore knitted sleeveless sweaters and twill type shirts. He smoked a pipe and always had a scent of workshop and pipe tobacco about him even though he was clean and well kept. He wouldn't have looked out of place presenting a countryside TV programme like 'One man and his dog'. He was never without an overcoat, and despite not being a huge man, Dad assured me there would be very few men who would consider tangling with him, ever. Not that he was aggressive at all, he had a very polite almost apologetic nature that bordered on awkwardness when invited in, or offered a cup of tea. He would do anything handy for us and expect nothing in return. I think Mum managed to get him to have some homemade cake with a brew once and gave him some to take home with him. He returned the favour tenfold, with cheeses from around the counties and sliced tongue and ham that he bought on his travels. He wore a flat cap which he would whip off in a flash if Mum appeared. He'd stand there wringing it, all embarrassed as he handed over whatever he had brought us from his adventures on the cricket circuit.

If from time to time his motorbike ever broke down, he would never take it to be repaired. He would strip it down himself and put right whatever had gone wrong. If it required a part replacing, he'd make it on his lathe, as bought in parts were rubbish and made of inferior materials. Dad would shake his head laughing when telling us stories about what he'd been up to, but it was always with admiration at his wonderful mechanical abilities.

Back at chez Hogarth we are now approaching the 'only for special occasions' front lounge. I was sent in there when Mum finally tired of me playing football in the back living room. I was not allowed to take my full sized ball as there were valuable ornaments on the mantelpiece and on top of the china cabinet. I was restricted to a ping-pong ball which had much less breakage potential. My trick was to throw it up against the wall and take the rebound on my chest before letting it drop onto my thigh. I would knee it back into the air, then let it drop and trap it on the carpet before clipping and bending it halfway up the curtains in the bay window. None of the imaginary goal keepers ever got anywhere near a single shot.

4. UP THE WOODEN HILL TO BEDFORDSHIRE

So to the first floor, and the slumber accommodation of our cosy family nest. The staircase had the usual traditional bannister and candy twirl spindles, and there was a left turn at the top, and then two more steps that led to the full landing. There was a skylight into the attic on the ceiling that had coloured stained glass. I was convinced I could see faces in the glass peering down at me. Especially if I was upstairs on my own. First on the right at the top of the stairs was the bathroom. It was small, had a bath, washbasin and a wall mounted two bar electric heater. There was a tiny airing cupboard with a lagged hot water tank and huge immersion heater switch with 'On' and 'Off' in red letters on a white background to assist you with your choice. One bar on the wall heater was plenty, according to Dad, even when it was minus seven outside, which it often was in winter. The years sixty two and sixty three, were perishingly cold. The floor was tiled lino, and caused instant cramp if you stood on it barefoot between November and February. A towel from the airing cupboard thrown down to stand on was my solution. There was a miniscule separate toilet located between the bathroom and the doorway to my bedroom. Very handy if I required night time wees. I never glanced up at the skylight whilst on night wee patrol, for fear some grotesque face would be watching my every move with twisted angry features.

I remember when we had the bathroom and loo redecorated one winter. It was a big deal, and a major joint family decision as to the patterns we picked for each location. We had about ten sample wallpaper books to wade through. They were massive and weighed a ton. Dad was in charge of lifting them onto the table and turning the pages when we had pondered each weary looking example for way too long. I wasn't a patient child. If it's hideous, just turn the page, and let's have a crack at the next one. I regularly had my hand smacked for trying to speed up the mind numbingly slow procedure.

"Just wait a minute, David, will you? We haven't decided on this one yet. Stop being in such a rush all the time."

Haven't decided? It looks like someone's been sick and then tried to mop it up with a cloth, I would think to myself. Finally we found one for the bathroom that was a complex swirly pattern of greens, blues, purples and golds that looked like someone had designed it whilst having a drug induced bad trip. I often wondered where my migraine problems originated. Probably lying in a red hot bath, trying to see pictures in the patterns on the wallpaper. The toilet paper (the stuff to go on the walls, not the tissue sort for mucky colon cleaning) was equally complex in colour and form. I seem to remember it was black, brown, orange, red and gold. Surprisingly, it wasn't as horrific as it sounds, and I would happily trace a route around the squiggles and swirls on the paper with my finger whilst I sat dropping a few logs off in the pond.

Next door to this was my sanctuary. The back twin bedroom that was my little den. Two single beds, one on each side of the room, a modern free-standing single wardrobe, a four drawer oak chest of drawers, and my small toy cupboard, which was a strange non-descript little unit that had two internal shelves and was painted a memorable distressed pale green. Its purpose, was to help keep the room tidy and not scattered liberally with neck breaking toys. On top of the drawers was my fort and a host of medieval toy knights. There was also a drawbridge, portcullis, look-out turrets, and an inner courtyard for very one-sided sword fight battles that featured my favourite knight, whose shield bore a distinctive red cross. From the number of enemies he slaughtered mercilessly, I can safely assume his red cross didn't have a compassionate medical connection. I have only ever slept walked twice in my life. Once, when I decided to get out of bed and swipe the fort and everything else on top of the drawers clean off with a crash onto the floor. Perhaps my own early protest against blood thirsty enactments of battle, involving the hacking to pieces of countless humans for greedy gain. The other occasion was in my thirties, when I woke up from an alcohol fuelled drunken slumber, to find myself standing flat against my bedroom wall with my nose inches from the light switch.

I slept in the bed closest to the toilet side of the room for easy night time pee excursions. I did sleep in the other bed from time to time just to mix things up a bit. This did drive Mum nuts, as it meant putting all fresh bedding on to the spare bed. The main draw on this side of the room was a dangling pale brown platted light-cord switch, that had a Bakelite egg shaped push bar on off mechanism. It enabled me the luxury of being able to switch my light off from the comfort of my own bed. I regularly lay swinging it back and forth until I nodded off, enjoying the slap it made in the palm of my hand. On one occasion I decided to dismantle the Bakelite black egg switch. This resulted in me receiving a jolt of electricity severe enough to have me quickly reassemble the thing, and hope that Mum wouldn't notice my newly blackened face and spikey smouldering hair. It's no wonder I'm as daft as a brush really, is it?

This swinging cord arrangement had other entertainment benefits. Namely, it enabled my best pal John and me to wrap Action Man around it like Tarzan swinging on a vine, and from the bed opposite hurl darts at him as he swung perilously over the crocodile infested creek. Several hits could dislodge him and send him to a horrible death in the jaws of the merciless river monsters. The darts stuck into his plastic flesh quite easily but there were many throws that missed and peppered the wallpaper to leave a bewildering pattern of tiny holes. I convinced Mum it was woodworm for quite a while, then received a clip round the ear when she walked in once during an Action Man arrow onslaught.

"What do you two think you're doing? Woodworm eh? I'll give you woodworm David if I ever catch you throwing darts at your toys and the wall again."

"I'm not sure you can give me woodworm actually, Mum, as I'm not made of wood."

I received a standard clipped ear for my insolence.

The next door along from my room was Mum and Dad's. The double bedroom at the front. It was the sort of size that hotel sites would label as, 'a cosy double'. In the alcoves were two lovely old matching wardrobes. Shaped tops to the double doors like blancmange moulds, and tiny locks with equally small antiquated keys. The top of the wardrobes behind the moulding was a favourite spot for Mum to think she had hidden Christmas presents from me. She hadn't figured on me bouncing on the bed like a trampoline to get enough height to take a sneaky peek. I had but a fraction of a second to take in the view and make my conclusions. I also had to quickly get back into my room to pretend I was bouncing on my own bed when I heard her cursing and coming upstairs to murder me again. I have been murdered so many times, that I can only assume my soul formerly belonged to a cat.

The highly polished graining to the wood held the images of what I decided were the heads of elephants. I felt that they looked wise and kind, but was unsure as to what they were doing on the front of my parents' wardrobes. There was a male wardrobe which was slightly bigger and was Dads'. The smaller one was for Mum and it had a great deal more in there in the way of fashion statements. The bed had a button back headboard that had two side table attachments that swung in over the bed so you could rest your cup of tea and book on there very nicely, thank you very much. Real posh and cutting edge for the mid-sixties. I remember how lovely it was at Christmas when we had broken up from school but Dad was still going to work right up to Christmas Eve. He was up early to catch the bus to Preston at seven thirty. Before he left he would make Mum a cup of tea and take it up to her in bed. He would make me one too, because I would always wake up when I heard him getting ready and going in the loo and bathroom. I would get into bed with Mum and we would read our books and drink tea while poor old Dad went out with his brolly in the pouring rain to catch his bus.

As well as the twin wardrobes, there was a matching dressing table too. It was also elegantly shaped and grand in appearance. In the centre was a huge oval mirror that was on a tilting mechanism. I once decided inexplicably to push the top of the mirror away from me hard, to see how far it tilted. The bottom of the mirror hit me flush on the chin and sent me flying backwards on to the bed.

Fortunately neither I nor the mirror came to any serious harm. I have a feeling that the sniggering elephants had something to do with it. Before Mum appeared to investigate what all the noise was about, I was able to reposition the mirror and relocate my swollen lower jaw bone just in time.

"What was that bang I heard, David? You haven't broken something have you?"

Err? Probably, yes, my lower mandible, Mother, I thought whilst shaking my head and keeping my chin down.

"You look mighty guilty young man, are you sure?"

I now nodded furiously, still unable to speak because of my expanding jaw line.

"Well just be careful and behave will you David, please? And why is that mirror vibrating?"

I shrugged my shoulders and slunk out of the room before I could be quizzed any further. I don't think Mum would have bought my elephant story for a minute. She did pretty much buy all my stories, and I have a feeling she knew when I was making stuff up, even before I did.

The final room at the end of the landing was my sister Kathryn's. It had a single bed and bedside cabinet, a matching single wardrobe and a three drawer dresser with mirror (non-tilting). There was a wall mounted display shelf unit that she kept little Beatrix Potter ornaments on, along with a multitude of Robertson's gollywog figures that you collected by eating copious amounts of jam and marmalade. For proof of purchase, you were required to send in the label on the jars to claim your pottery reward. They had the figures doing all sorts. Football, Tennis, playing in a jazz band. Mine and Kate's diet was predominantly jam and marmalade, but we had hundreds of pot figures so diabetes and obesity seemed a small price to pay for such finely crafted figurines. I am pretty certain that Robertson's main thrust of their campaign was increase profits, and not to instigate racism.

My sister was a regular recipient of the butt end of many a younger brother's prank. These consisted of secreting joke shop items in her bed. I was spared the usual thick ear until overstepping the mark with a very life-like plastic dog turd. I had got away with written warnings for snakes, mice and spiders. Fake ones of course, but still hilariously realistic all the same.

Her screams and cursing when she climbed into bed every night was music to my swollen and continually clipped ears.

We weren't always in battle mode my sister and I, we did both enjoy the top twenty count down on a Sunday teatime. Hosted more often than not by 'That's right, pop pickers' Alan Freeman... 'Not half'. I use to love hearing him do his non-stop run through of the hits from number twenty to number one without taking a breath. Then we would sit there on Kate's bed swaying to the rhythm and clicking our fingers whilst singing all the wrong lyrics to that weeks' top of the pops. Well, I did. Even back then my desire to be silly was overwhelming. Why sing the official lyrics to anything, when you can make up hilarious ridiculous ones of your own. Kate would frown and shake her head at me, and occasionally punch me on the arm if I overstepped the mark with vulgarity. My arm took quite a pounding every Sunday.

Our transistor radio was the height of modern technology, despite needing two of us to carry it. It was about the size of a corn flakes box and judging from its weight, was lined with industrial lead. This, I think, was to stop the wicked radio waves penetrating your skull and frying your brain. Instead, the music of the sixties pop chart fulfilled that role nicely. It tempted you over to the dark side, with tales of rebellious love, and a general hatred of anything to do with the establishment. The front had a jazzy white grill which housed the speaker. Above that, was the clear plastic strip that had the red pointer you moved along with the big dial to tune into your favourite station? A smaller dial was the volume control, and when turned up to the maximum setting, you could almost hear people singing. Both of the two knobs were white, with milled grooved edges and gold shiny fronts. The casing was turquoise blue leather effect plastic, and there was a carrying handle across the top should you be tempted to take your music box to the beach or the park and thereby make a complete fool of yourself. I made a complete fool of myself regularly, and on many occasions, without the need or help from a transistor radio.

pony ride at the Pleasure Beach, 1963

5. BARKING MAD PUPPY LOVE

One of my very first recollections ever at the family home, was the arrival of another little one, a puppy. My sister didn't stand a chance in the 'who can stroke doggy the most' competition. It was like my damned hand had been super glued to her head (the puppy's head, not my sister's). Wherever she went so did I. She was named Judy. My suggestions of Gnasher, Lucifer and Stingray were ignored. Even my brilliant idea that we could shorten Lucifer if needs be went unheeded after they pointed out that Judy was a bitch. Bit harsh, I thought, she was lovely. I went on hunger strike and refused to speak. It lasted till lunch time. I broke my protest when I reluctantly asked Mum for a sandwich. Now Mum, god bless her, did her utmost to protect Judy from my stroke addiction, but it was like trying to keep seagulls away from a dropped bag of chips. She would even take her into the kitchen and claim she was sleepy and needed to rest in her little basket. Nonsense woman, look at those pleading sad little puppy eyes. It's clear to me, at least, she needs non-stop stroking.

"Come on now, leave her be for a while. She's had enough. Go and kick a ball around, or draw, or read a book or something".

"A book!?... A book!!? Have you lost your mind, woman?" I thought.

As I kicked my ball relentlessly against the back wall outside, all that was on my mind was how to sneak back inside to continue with my puppy stroking. Leave the back gate open, so Mum will think I'm out in the back alley. Quick peep through the back window to make sure the coast is clear. In through the outhouse door, then pull the kitchen door shut to ensure privacy, and bingo. My hand must have been millimetres from my flat headed reluctant best friend when,...

"LEAVE... HER... ALONE! I won't tell you again, David, go outside and kick your damn ball about, but LEAVE... HER... ALONE. If you carry on like this she won't let you stroke her at all."

"Okay, Okay, I'm going, I'm going, keep your wig on."

"You'll get a clip round the ear in a minute you cheeky monkey, go on, out, and keep that ball down, don't go booting it into Aunty Mary's."

Keep it down?! Booting it?! Have you gone mad Mother, and forgotten the levels of footballing skills I possess? Two minutes later, I was stood at the fence between our gardens shouting,...

"Aunty Mary, please can I have my ball back?"

I made the fatal mistake of glancing at our back living room window. Mum was shaking her fist at me with gritted teeth. She looked more than mildly irritated.

"It bounced up off the back step," was my mouthed explanation, as I accompanied my feeble excuse with vague pointing gestures and a looping trajectory demo of the ball with my arm.

"I'll murder you", was my Mum's mouthed reply through the glass.

By the time I had my ball back and finally went in, Mum had forgotten all about murdering me.

"What did I tell you about not kicking it too hard?"

"I know, sorry, it flew off the corner of the back step. I can't help having a rocket of a left foot, can I?"

"I'll rocket you, sunny Jim. Just be more careful. What did Aunty Mary say?"

"Same as you, just be careful, David, keep it down. We don't want any broken windows do we?"

"Quite right, no we don't. Go and wash your hands, there's some lunch ready."

Drama over, no murdering, and by some miracle of my Mum's inexhaustible patience, I was in the clear again.

Speaking of murdering, there was one lunchtime when I had, as usual, been woofing down my lunch at break neck speed, so I could get back to stroking puppy or booting a ball around. At my last swallow of grub I realised that I may have bitten off more than I could chew. I swallowed again and nothing happened. Just this strange empty gulping sound. Then I drew in breath and that wasn't working either. I took a drink of water, and that just spilled back out of my mouth.

Whoops, I was dying! My ears started to ring, but I didn't have time to answer them as I was choking. My Mum and sister were in the kitchen and I wandered in trying to look as calm as you can when you are seconds away from death. Mums are cool when it comes to the life saving of their own children.

"Oh my God, David, what is it!?"

I pointed quite urgently to my bunged up cake hole and tried to hang on to my bulging eyeballs and not pass out. In a flash I was spun round and bent over. I don't remember to this day ever being hit harder than my Mum whacked me that day. I was very relieved to see a lump of lunch the size of a small planet shoot out onto the kitchen floor. Once my eyes stopped spinning and settled back into my head I got a severe ticking off for not chewing my food properly and eating too quickly.

Fortunately for me, Mum had a real keen eye when it came to spotting offspring dying as a result of un-chewed gluttony. Her knowledge of thumping children in the middle of the back to help them not die was second to none.

Right, time for a well chewed quick spot of lunch, methinks, then I know someone who will be just dying to have her cute little flat puppy head stroked again. Oh, and thanks Mum, you saved my life. Twice, at least. Once, when I tried to swallow a cannonball sized lump of masticated braised steak, and secondly, when I began to give up on life after you passed away.

Staying in touch from beyond, and watching over me from above, that's some pretty neat trick. Mothers are very clever people, don't you know?

6. THE THEORY OF EVERYTHING, OR NOTHING, OR SOMETHING

I can't be certain of my age when I very nearly stroked a puppy to death, but by the process of elimination and poor mathematics, I've arrived at somewhere between three and four years old. I once asked a young Mum how old her two kids were. "Seven and six," was the un-engaging short response. You could have got a dog licence for the same money I thought. I patted them both on the head. So, stroking the puppy is pretty much the first memory I have at home. I remember coming out with stories about Judy when we were all reminiscing as a family once. Mum was amazed at my powers of recollection. It's only remembering Mum, It's not like I've discovered the secrets of the universe or anything (Or have I?) (No). I'm sure if I had I would have written it down somewhere and put it in my bedside cabinet. I was in there the other day and it definitely wasn't there. That's annoying isn't it? Putting stuff down, and then forgetting where you put it. I bet the same thing happened to Stephen Hawking when he was a kid.

"Where's my sub-atomic particle notebook for God's sake, Mum!?... Mum!?"

"What, Stephen? I'm in the Kitchen."

"Where's my sub-atomic particle notebook?"

"Where you left it probably."

"It's not. I always leave it next to my Rupert the Bear annual and it's not there."

"Well when did you have it last? Have you looked in the cupboard where you keep your theory on something or nothing? Or under your bed with your reflections on the space time continuous."

"Continuum! Continuum, Mother! What is a space time continuous for Christ's sake?"

"I don't know, something that keeps going and doesn't give up I guess? Don't get shirty with me young man or I'll come up there and clip your ear for you. I'm not the one with the silly IQ."

"Well where else would it be then for God's sake? Have you been moving my stuff around again?"

"No, I haven't Stephen. Just look. It's probably right under your damn nose somewhere. It'll be in your satchel I bet. Or maybe, when you close your bedroom door, it just shifts into another dimension."

"Oh ha ha ha, very funny Mother, such a big help in a crisis…. Wait a minute, what did you just say?"

"It'll be in your satchel."

"No not that, the bit about another dimension."

"Oh I don't know, I just thought with all these Quarks, and Higgs Boson particles whizzing around, that maybe stuff just disappears for a while, and then pops back unannounced, you know, a bit like your Gran does from time to time."

And there it is, there you have it. Not only the secrets of the Universe revealed, but that's you bang to rights, Hawking. Your notebook, by the way, was down the side of your bed all the time. Right where you dropped it when you nodded off trying to write the theory of something or other, or nothing or something.

We are all just a collection of particles obeying the laws of physics. Good old scientists eh? They know everything. If ever you needed a succinct and joyless way to describe the human existence, then there it is. It does have a nice ring to it though. It sums everything up nice and neatly in a way that makes you hope your life will be short and sweet. But really? Where is the spirit of the Universe in that mathematical summary of life? I'll tell you where. It's on holiday on some fantastic beach looking at azure blue water, feeling the breeze on its face, the sand beneath its feet, sipping cocktails, checking out the scenery and having a right old knees up, that's where.

I think we should add a bit more mystery and what if to the equation. Let's alter it a touch and bring a glimmer of hope to the all but faithless and cynical. Namely,...me.

'We are the spirit and soul of the Universe, here to light infinity'. Not quite as snappy or to the point. But then neither is life. Well not unless you happen to be a collection of particles obeying the laws of physics. I was one myself until my Mum passed away.

Call yourself a Cosmologist Mr.Hawking? Russell Grant blows you out of the water, pal. He once told me, through the medium of newspaper horoscopes, that I would make a decision about something or other, or nothing or something, and meet someone who would give me some advice about something or other, or nothing or something. Less than six months after I read that, it all came true. A bit.

I am going to lay the blame squarely at the door of the late great Stephen Hawking at this point. During my thirties, it was he who lured me into purchasing 'A Brief History of Time'.

It is lovely to think that dear old Professor Hawking will now be walking and talking in robust full health somewhere. I would imagine he will be having words with the big fella and asking why he was hindered so much here on earth.

"Because you were too smart for your own good, young man. That's why. I couldn't have you simplifying billions of years of creative genius into one equation."

"Fair point. How close was I, Boss?"

"Let's just say, you should have listened to your Mum."

Up to this point, I had just been happily tootling through life, half- heartedly believing in God, baby Jesus, Angels, Heaven and Hell, horoscopes, and then as if by magic, out of the blue, I'm drawn to this book about space and time. The origins of the Universe. It really made me think. Remember, my Mum and Dad used to call me Bird Brain. I began to question life, the Universe, and our place within it.

I do however approve of how you referred to yourself as 'Something of a dreamer'. You have become part of the dream itself now, and those dreams of yours are still with us. We have a lot in common you and I Stevie boy. You were a genius, and I'm as daft as a brush. You weren't a Gemini by any chance? Check out Russell Grant's horoscope page, and don't be too quick to judge. Just having your maths 'A' level, doesn't give you the right to go round dismissing the existence of a creator and the influence of the stars. I got a 'C' in Art, but I don't go round slagging Van Gogh off, telling everyone he painted by numbers. An open heart and an empty mind is what's required, Stevie boy. "Use your imagination David", Mum would say. "Something will turn up."

7. OH I WISH IT COULD BE CHRISTMAS

One very magical Christmas Eve, my imagination went into overdrive and something very wonderful turned up in full HD and technicolour. I had a dream that I was watching myself asleep in bed, observing from a kind of out of body perspective. My room was dark, but because the sky outside was full of snow, I could make out all the furniture and features easily. It had snowed heavily, and the view out of my bedroom window looked across neighbours' gardens to the rooftops of the houses opposite. There was a wide expanse of sky that glowed of Christmas. It was still and silent. Huge glistening snowflakes swirled like giant feathers in the crisp air, down towards a thick white carpet that had already settled on the ground. There, they disappeared into the rest of the sparkling mass. Suddenly the silence was broken by the faintest of sounds. The sound of sleigh bells. I glanced down at myself to see if I had heard them. I stirred a little, but turned over and remained asleep. The bells again, this time louder, and getting closer. I looked again, and to my relief I had begun to wake up and hear what every young child dreams of on Christmas Eve. A dream that lives in your heart. My observing spirit jumped back into me. I was groggy though and unsure of what I'd heard. There it was again, louder and closer. I could barely bring myself to step out of bed and dare to look. What if? What if what? What if I pulled back my curtain and there was nothing to see, what if I was hearing the sound of sleigh bells, but I wouldn't actually see what my heart was dreaming of. Well there was only one way to find out? I leapt out of bed and grasped the edge of my curtain. The bells were not quite as loud now, moving away, fading. I almost didn't want to look for fear of disappointment. I pulled back the curtain and my eyes quickly scanned everywhere at once. I panicked, because all I could see were snowflakes. Huge swirling snowflakes against the dark night sky. Fading. The fear and panic in my head turned to tears.

I can't see him, I can't see him.

The bells were almost gone and I had to strain to hear them. I rubbed my eyes hard to clear them of tears, but they came back as fast as I rubbed. Then suddenly I saw it. Much higher in the sky than I was looking, the twinkling of tiny lights and a sleigh. It was being pulled by a huge host of reindeer. It wasn't as I had imagined it in my mind, but there it was, nonetheless. I could see it clearly as it moved faster across the night sky. I could hear the joyous sound of sleigh bells. I could even make out the red of Santa's suit and the silhouette shape of the sleigh. His suit was a crimson red. His intent was clear. He was busy, and had a great deal to do. The sleigh moved further on across the sky. I daren't even breathe as it would mist up the view I had. I could still hear the bells as it finally disappeared out of view behind the rooftops opposite. I was smiling widely, because I couldn't believe what I had just seen. But I had seen it, and now I could believe.

I remember feeling so happy and content that I had the evidence with my own eyes as I settled back under the covers. I could sleep soundly, and tell everyone about it tomorrow. What a fantastic tale to tell on Christmas morning.

When I woke up I had the most wonderful feeling inside me. On the other single bed in my room was a white pillow case stuffed with colourful presents. I was four or five years old at the time. These were harsh winters. Ice on the inside of my bedroom window as well as outside. I remember one particularly severe winter being pulled across the ice on Stanley Park Lake. I was on a homemade sledge that my Dad had constructed from wooden crates (I wasn't just being dragged bodily at the end of a rope, you understand?). Whilst this was great fun for myself and my sister Kate, I do have to question my Father's judgement regarding the health and safety aspect. We were right out in the middle of the lake! I cannot believe my inflated armbands would have saved me had we come across a less than sturdy area of winter's grip. After our sledging escapades had thankfully ended without incident, we were walking back around the outside of the lake, when Judy, our flat headed Cocker Spaniel puppy, stepped off the edge of the path onto an area of slushy ice. She disappeared straight through and resurfaced with an expression on her face that I can only best describe as 'what the dickens!?' For a few panicky moments she thrashed around trying to get back to the edge and onto the path. Dad finally managed to grab her by the scruff of the neck and yank her out. She was in total shock, shivering like an orphaned match seller from a Charles Dickens novel, and the days of yore. Fortunately, we had a blanket on the sledge to stop us getting splinters in our arses. That had to be Mum's idea. We wrapped her frozen little face and shivering torso in the blanket and headed for the Park gates at high speed. It was one of those horrible frightening moments when you think you are about to lose someone. We got her home in record time and she enjoyed fifteen minutes of fireside recovery with us all rubbing her like crazy with towels and telling her what a good little dog she was. Good?! Good!? She jumped in the lake, for God's sake, like some nut job kamikaze puppy. I did daft stuff every day, but I was just a bird brain. I started to well up, I'd nearly lost my little dog.

"Aw come on, she's okay now, look she's fine, she's all warm and dry again. Look, she's even wagging her tail." Mum said, with a comforting arm around me. My spiritual flat headed canine pal noticed how upset I was and came over sniffing at me wagging her little stump of a docked tail. No wonder we had a bond. Mum convinced me she wasn't going to die, and after some feasting from my selection box, I was back to my 'daft as a brush' old self again, stroking the head of my best friend sitting together by the fire. As we sat there, she minding her own business, me stroking her head flat like a nutter, we just looked into the flames and wondered what lay ahead. Besides tea of course. After a while, I stopped stroking her. When I did, a few seconds later, she lifted her head up off the rug and rested it on my knee. I stopped staring into the flames and glanced down at her. As soon as I did, she looked up at me with her big brown puppy eyes, and the message sank in.

"I get it... too much stroking, huh?"

She gave a half- hearted yawn, closed her eyes, and put her head back down on my knee. I never stroked her again. Well, not for five minutes I didn't.

Besides, there were many other adventures that lay ahead for us. Cattle rustling in the lounge for one. Judy played the part of a young steer, and I, the very handy rope wielding ranch hand whose job it was to round her up. I used the cord from my dressing gown fashioned into a lasso. It was another adventure that ended up with my Mum threatening to murder me.

"David, sometimes you know, you can be such an idiot," Mum said, as she frantically tried to cut through my cattle restraining knots.

Well, I'm sure you get the picture? But back to all that winter wonderment, and the crazy excited run up to Christmas! From about September the fifth onwards, to be precise. Back to school, and all the talk was of who was getting what, and how many of them. You must have a kid in your memory like that. You know, the one who was getting every game and toy that was ever invented from A to Z. No matter what you would say you were getting, they would always be ready to trump it ten times over. They could barely wait for you to finish speaking to butt in with, "ANYWAY, I'm getting the Grand Prix 60,000 all seater stadium Champion of Champions De-Luxe put that in your pipe and smoke it version. So there." All I had said was, "I've asked for a Scalextric as my big present."

"Yeah well, I'm getting a jump jet, an aircraft carrier, a Lamborghini, a machine gun, Walrus skin football boots (didn't exist), a watch that lets me travel through time (and back), a Tiger, a swimming pool, two electric guitars, a Subbuteo, oh yeah and some new pyjamas."

The sad thing is, sometimes you'd believe them, then walk home kicking anything that you could get away with without hurting your foot. I usually hurt my foot. Then as it got much closer to Christmas, mid-October, you would ramp up the pressure and start dropping a hundred hints a day as to what it was you wanted. Anything that was met with, "You'll just have to wait and see" was in the bag, anything that got. "We aren't made of money, David," was filed under 'no chance'.

When December arrived and decorations started to appear, it was all you could do not to throw up in excitement. Still, Mum would hold us back on tight reins. It was a Hogarth family tradition that the Christmas tree went up about two weeks before the big day. Usually the ritual took place on a Sunday afternoon. It would always be grey, cold and miserable, which was a strange choice for a Christmas tree.

The decorations and the tree were stored in the loft. It required an organised military operation to retrieve them. When the clock struck two and our lunches had gone down, it was time to get the small step ladder from the garage (we didn't have a large one) (step ladder, not garage). Despite its small stature, great care had to be taken not to kill anyone or break anything during its journey to the bathroom. Getting it up the stairs required many delicate adjustments not to scrape the wallpaper. The insanely tiny opening to the loft was located behind the door in the ceiling, and only large enough for yours truly to fit through. It was a chance for me to rise and shine. Quite literally. I could prove that I had a string to my bow that didn't have the word idiot in its DNA. The plan was Dad would ascend first to push the loft cover up and out of the way. I hoped he would also disturb and scare away any spiders, mice, rats, bats, squirrels, pigeons, owls, bees, wasps, foxes, and evil spirits. Lofts are scary places, with many a hidden danger.

The worst thing that ever actually occurred, was there may be a tiny bit of cobweb dangling down from the cover. The family torch, with a beam that was barely detectable to the human eye, was used to shine into the Cathedral sized loft. I was given map co-ordinates by my Dad, and a stern warning not to stand anywhere other than on the beams.

Once I had pulled myself up into the vast black pyramid, I realised lowering myself back down would be a lot trickier. Possibly life threatening. I amazed not only my family, but myself, when I failed to fall through the ceiling and keep my balance whilst stepping across the beams. Boxes and tree successfully passed through the opening, I lowered myself back down to the top of the small ladder. My legs dangled blindly for a few seconds until they were low enough for Dad to guide my feet onto the top rung. Mission accomplished. The family Hogarth could now spend the afternoon saying, "Aw, I'd forgotten about that one," as we unwrapped hundreds (fifty or so at the most) individually wrapped tree decorations that had survived the boxed hibernation.

First things first though. The leaf of the table had to be pulled out, and a rug-like table cloth placed on top to avoid scratches from the Christmas tree tripod legs. Branches were straightened downwards to a horizontal position so that it actually resembled the shape of a tree. The top branch was pointed towards the heavens in readiness for the fairy to be lowered into place. I always had a sneaky look up her dress despite having no plausible reason to do so. I was only five or six, but even then I was clearly fascinated by female legs. They were slim and shapely. I remember Mum frowning and shaking her head.

We had two big square boxes with decorations in, and a massive bird's nest of tangled lights that Dad would curse at every Christmas. He couldn't understand how they were in this mess after winding them up neatly the previous year. They appear to mutate once stored away safely. Like a writhing mass of young snakes jostling for position. It just didn't make any sense.

"What has happened here? These were all wound up so they would be easy to unravel. You haven't had these out David, have you?"

Then, the first big test to see if the lights were still

working. A collective holding of our breath, and in went the plug. Working, fantastic. Back slapping and cheery smiles all round. Everything cold and grey and miserable would very soon be gone at the flick of a switch.

Next, the main event. The unwrapping and placement of the decorations. I was only allowed a minor role in this operation. Mum was chief placer, Kate and I did a lot of pointing. Dad went into the lounge and read the Sunday paper. Perhaps my crushing of ornaments in the past, as I ham-fistedly took the tissue off had something to do with my junior role. I was however, one of the finest, if not, the finest, pointers in our family. By using my eyes, and looking, I could see areas of the tree that were devoid of decorations, and almost without hesitation, or fear of ridicule, I would point vaguely in those directions. As my confidence grew, I would accompany my unspecific arm waving with the word, "There", which at times was rewarded with a bauble being placed somewhere quite close to, or fairly near, that general area to which I had pointed. The sense of achievement was overwhelming. Such heart-warming success would prompt me to help myself to another segment of chocolate orange. I was the master at quickly grabbing a piece unseen, and getting the whole thing into my gob without being detected.

"I think that's quite enough chocolate for now young man, you've just had your lunch," the back of my Mum's head would say. How did she do that? Silly noisy orange tin foil wrapper.

"You'll be sick, just save some for later or you'll have none left over Christmas." This, if I knew my Mum well, was just another ruse. There would be more chocolate come Christmas day morning than Willy Wonka had got stored at his newly extended large warehouse. Or at the very least, two selection boxes that featured some, or not any, of my favourite chocolate bars. This did not matter to any child on Christmas Day. You would heartily attack anything within the box simply because it was Christmas. Bars you would never usually dream of entertaining would now seem irresistible due to the sinister Christmas effect. Even the possibility of an upset stomach did little to stop the craving.

Some carried more potential risk than others. Fry's chocolate cream, one whole bar, possible vomit potential if consumed after scrambled eggs with cheese and H.P. sauce. Toffee Crisp, quite small and a touch salty, safe. Fry's Turkish delight, if eaten with twiglets, vomit potential high. Throw in a tangerine and some peanuts, and projectile vomit was guaranteed. The opportunity was there to gorge on chocolate from five a.m. until you were violently sick, which usually clashed with Mum making dinner or watching the Queen's speech. Possibly the most boring ten minutes of television that is ever broadcast (when you are a child). Apologies your Majesty, but when you're waiting to watch 'Jason and the Argonauts' for the fifth time that Christmas, a monologue of what you have been up to for twelve months should be broadcast at ten to bedtime to help people nod off.

Back to the tree. Now looking pleasantly laden with decorations and lights. The big plug in moment had arrived again. Nothing. Plug out. Plug back in. Still nothing.

"Why does this happen every year?" Dad asked, gently.

"Could be the fuse that's gone, that's all." Mum would say.

Buy some new ones maybe, I would mumble under my breath. These things look like Thomas Edison's first attempt at night school to make a series of miniature lighting enhancements for the festive season of Noel. Dad actually got them at skinny Ellis's bike shop on Whitegate Drive. Yes, bike shop, and yes, alarmingly skinny.

Our tree was lovely though, when all the placing and lighting was complete. I use to love coming up our street when it was dark in the evening in winter. About halfway up you could see it. The lounge curtains would be open. There were only a few humans alive with the strength to shut them. Mum and Gran were two of them.

It was perched on top of the china cabinet with the tripod base sitting in a cut glass fruit bowl. The legs were secured inside the bowl with rolled up newspaper stuffed firmly around them. Tinsel was laid on top like the whipped cream finale of a newsprint trifle. It worked though, and our proud little silver tree with much loved ornaments and lights was there to warm your heart as you got close to home on dark, cold, and wet December nights.

I use to go into the lounge regularly, switch the tree lights on, and stand in the dark with my eyes screwed up a little, just staring in wonder at how great it looked. It filled me with Christmas. I felt lucky. Lucky that my Mum and Dad were parents who cared and loved us. Lucky that we were always laughing and looking forward to things. Lucky that our home was warm and safe and we were always eating wonderful things my Mum would bake and cook. I would well up with tears because of how lucky I was. Despite the fact that I was daft as a brush.

"Not for five minutes can you be serious David, can you? You always have to spoil it by saying something silly."

"Sorry, Mum."

When it came to Christmas Eve, I can remember the excitement and anticipation becoming almost too much to bear. I would walk around singing, "It's Christmas Eve, It's Christmas Eve, and people come to stay and leave." I had no idea what the second line of the song was, so I just made up anything that rhymed. We had things like, "And people love to sing and grieve"... "Put on your hat, roll up your sleeve." (just the one sleeve, you'll note?)... "No time for tears, no time to plead."

It would be at this point that my Mum would step in with, "Alright, alright, just calm down a bit, you're getting all giddy and silly now. Just sit down and cool off, you'll be making yourself sick if you carry on like that. Why don't you read a book?"

"A book? A book?!"... *Have you gone mad Mother? It's Christmas Eve for crying out loud. I'm doing all I can here to work myself into a frenzy so that at bedtime tonight I don't so much fall asleep as pass out, and you're suggesting that I should read a book!?*

"Yes, you should read 'A Christmas Carol' by Charles Dickens. It's a fantastic story, and very Christmassy. You'd enjoy it."

How right you were Mum, sadly though, not for many years would I realise it is one of the most wonderful stories ever written. A story, by some silly old geezer, about carols at Christmas. You must be joking. I'm busy wearing myself out making up lyrics of my own, thank you very much.

"It's Christmas Eve, Its Christmas Eve, a thread of life, with much to weave."

Oi, Dickens, out of my head please, I'm on a roll here, pal.

"It's Christmas Eve, it's Christmas Eve, let's sing a song and have some cheese." Nailed it.

This idiotic Christmas fuelled excitement would

continue right throughout the day. Interrupted only by the need for food and the toilet. A wee every half hour at least. The watching of any cartoon. Even very unfunny dreadful ones made in the 1930's. Stroking the dog. Assisting in food preparation. My role was to stay away from sharp knives and look at the Turkey. It was in a box in the outhouse thawing out. I was allowed to peel sprouts. I was a touch overzealous discarding the outer leaves which resulted in them ending up the size of peas. I was just making sure there were no dirty sprouts going in my belly on Christmas day. I was relieved of my duties after six sprouts. I knew which ones I'd be spooning onto my plate come the big feast. Then there was looking at the tree through squinted vision, and the watching of 'Ben-Hur' for five hours.

"It's the story of Christ, and there is a fantastic chariot race in it, you'll enjoy it," Mum would try to sell it. I would sit sulking with my arms folded pretending not to watch. After three and a half hours I had completely forgotten about 'The Magnificent Seven' on ITV. I now knew what I was going to be when I grew up. A chariot driver. I also knew what I wanted for Christmas next year. Four white Arabian horses with cool names. They would have the ability to run like the wind, or faster, if it was just breezy. I had to reluctantly admit that the film was okay, even though my eyes were dry and stinging from my unblinking world record. My previous best span of attention prior to this epic was 'Snow White and the Seven Dwarfs' with a run time of twenty nine minutes. I wasn't a patient child, or easily entertained, but that Ben-Hur chap was alright in my book. Jesus seemed like a nice lad too, although he wasn't in it much. I do remember it was cloudy and raining the day they nailed him to the cross. At one point in the film he does a stand-up routine on the top of a hill. He must have been good, as thousands turned up to listen. There was a fish and bread supper promised though, so that probably attracted a good few scroungers. At the part when he died in Ben-Hur, anyone who was poorly got better, the sun came out, and that was that. This didn't sit well with me because no-one seemed to be bothered about him getting nailed to a cross, stabbed in the side, and seven bells kicked out of him. The best bit though, was when the wheel on Masala's chariot bust, and he got trampled by all the other horses in the race. Served him right, he was cheating with excessive use of the whip. Ben-Hur goes into the changing rooms after the match, and tries to get Masala to see what a prick he's been. He's having none of it. He is now a crumpled broken bleeding mess of a Roman Army Commander. The fact he lost the race has really mashed his swede in. He pretends to be tough and refuses to let the surgeons chop his legs off to save him from bleeding to death. Thirty seconds later, he croaks. What a knob head.

There are more thorough and in depth reviews out there of this multi Oscar winning film should you care to read them. But if it's a five year old's take you're after, give it a watch. You will jump for joy when Masala gets trampled half to death. You may need a box of tissues though when Ben-Hur's Mum and Sister's eczema clears up. Spare a thought for Jesus too. He seemed very much to get the rough end of the stick for just trying to be caring and friendly towards everyone.

Okay, back to Christmas Eve afternoon. We've done the big movie. We're full of things we hate. Walnuts, Brazils, Tangerine segments with all pith removed, Dates, unsalted Peanuts from the shell, Turkish delight not covered in chocolate, Fig rolls, Ritz crackers and Twiglets.

"I think you need something sensible for tea, David, It's a big day tomorrow and you will be eating all day, knowing you. How does scrambled eggs on toast sound?'

Before I could even process what had been said I replied, "Yeah, sounds great." Scrambled eggs on toast? This was the eve of one of man's greatest historical events ever. The day that Santa flies around the world at the speed of light and deposits presents down your chimney, and we start the celebrations with egg on toast?

"Can I have some bacon with it Mum, please?"

"Okay, but just one slice, you'll need all your appetite for tomorrow's turkey."

My god! The turkey? I hadn't looked at it for hours.

"Okay, shall I check the turkey, Mum?"

"If you like? Don't touch it though. What do you keep going and looking at the turkey for?"

"Oh, you know, just making sure it's okay, thawing out and stuff." (Because I'm daft as a brush, Mum).

On the way into the outhouse, I also realised it was high time I stroked my dog's head again and squinted at the Christmas tree lights. I pulled the two sides of the cardboard box lid open and looked at the turkey. Then I closed the lid and went to stroke Judy's head, followed by a squint at the Christmas tree.

Fully scrambled up, it was now entering the phase when a decision needed to be made about what time I should go to bed. The answer was almost always, needlessly early. But why? I'd had a busy day squinting, stroking, singing, critiquing, eating and peeing, so by all accounts I should be exhausted. A sensible young man would do the decent thing and get an early night. (I remember banging my head against my bedroom wall last year in a desperate, failed, and painful bid to knock myself out on Christmas Eve).

"I think I'll turn in soon, Mum."

"It's half past four in the afternoon, David!"

"Yeah I know, but I'll have a bath and read for a bit."

"You won't sleep you know, it's far too early to be going to bed."

Right again of course, such knowledgeable creatures these Mothers. Then at about ten minutes to nine came a shout up the stairs.

"Are you alright up there? What was that loud banging noise?"

"Err yeah, I'm fine, it's ok, I just dropped my book... you know? The big heavy one."

8. SO THIS IS CHRISTMAS

At about twenty past eleven, and with an egg sized lump on the side of my skull, I finally nodded off. I was woken again a little while later, by what appeared to be my Father in his pyjamas putting a large rustling pillowcase on the spare bed. This was all a bit confusing. Even more so as my vision was impaired from head butting the wall again. Santa must have been already. So what is my Dad doing messing around with my sack full of Christmas happiness? Still cross-eyed and groggy from my self-inflicted head trauma, I was just about to shout out, "Oi you, what do you think you're doing?" when he turned and started to tip toe out of the room leaving my presents just where I could keep my blurred and swirling vision on them. He must have been checking Santa had got everything spot on.

Safe in the knowledge that my presents had arrived and been double checked, I blacked out for the rest of the evening and drifted off into a blissful coma. When I finally came round, I could tell it was morning. Not light, but not pitch black either. In the half- light, and even with double vision from a fractured skull, I could see that my sack of presents was just where I remembered. Should I be a good lad and wait a bit longer or should I...

"MUM! DAD! Can I open my presents now please? Its morning." I shouted at the top of my lungs. It wasn't a big house. A modest mid terraced home with three bedrooms.

"Yes, go on then, take them into Kate's room." Came the answer I'd hoped for.

It was a really nice thing we always did, Kate and I at Christmas. I'd climb into bed with her, we'd haul our pillow cases on to the bed, and then take it in turns to open a present each. We would laugh so much that Mum or Dad would shout, "Okay, Okay, just keep the noise down a bit you two, you'll wake the whole street up." It was great. The pile of stuff we had was fantastic. Not crazy expensive things, just really lovely presents that a very wise Mum and Dad knew we would love. As a gesture of love and appreciation, we would go downstairs and make Mum and Dad a truly awful cup of tea each. My role was to point at things and never carry anything. I was allowed to pass Kate the tray, which was snuggly located and stored in the gap between the fridge and kitchen cupboard. Right next to my favourite Christmas doggy, who was now sat up, yawning, wagging her tail.

Her home consisted of an open wooden basket, that either Dad, or Uncle Stan (not our real uncle) had constructed. Crude but effective. Judging by the state of the edges, tasty and chewable too. It was lined with a couple of smelly doggy blankets and a cushion for her little flat head. She was shut in the kitchen at night, which gave her some well-earned rest from head flattening. On the way back upstairs after pointing at things in the kitchen, I detoured into the front lounge to plug the tree lights in. It was never too early for a squinty stare at those twinkling beauties. In a moment of strange compulsion, I decided to go over and take a look at the nativity scene. It was on the coffee table with a lace doily beneath it to prevent scratching of course. It was good quality. All the characters actually resembled humans, apart from the animals. It was all nicely painted, and the figures had a comforting cold weight to them. Baby Jesus was a right little cutie pie. He was naked but for some swaddling underpants, which to my dismay, were not removable. My urge to stroke his head was strong. It's the baby Jesus you idiot! Not a Cocker Spaniel puppy, you can't go stroking his bonce on Christmas Day, for God's sake.

It was Christmas Day though, and technically his birthday. I laid him back in his manger and took two steps back before bowing in half to the waist and saying,

"Happy Birthday Sir, and a very Merry Christmas to you, your family, and all of those in Bethlehem and the surrounding areas."

I may have also tested how solid he was with my teeth before putting him back. I gave a final military style salute, and then resisted having a cow, sheep and donkey shootout with the three wise men. Having paid my respects to our Lord and Saviour, I squinted at the tree again for a few more seconds, then sprinted back upstairs to re-examine all of my presents in much greater detail.

Two of my favourites already were a Robot, and a Rocket Launcher. The Robot was about a foot tall and made of detailed coloured tin. It was mainly grey but had a front panel with flashing lights and whirling cogs. If you hit the chest panel at just the right spot with a rocket, it would burst open and the two barrel sized batteries would drop out and stop the advancing Robot in his tracks. This would prevent potential global Armageddon and the death of thousands in Bethlehem, and surrounding areas. God and Jesus shook my hand warmly, and hailed me a hero in the face of total destruction of the planet. They were so thrilled with me for all I'd done that they allowed me to address the masses with them. Our trio of speeches to the huge cheering crowd saw peace and goodwill return to all mankind that very morning. My God,... the turkey!

I was down the stairs and in the outhouse in a flash. Flaps open. Still there. Two finger prod of huge dead beast.

Good give in the flesh, thawing nicely. Flaps shut. Back to the Robot wars in my bedroom. The crowds were still going wild and cheering. Jesus frowned and threw me a "Where have you been?" look. "Turkey," I mouthed back, and he grinned knowingly, nodding his head with a thumbs up. I wasn't even high on Port and lemonade or chocolate yet.

Back upstairs in my room, I lovingly admired all my other presents. I got a selection box, new pyjamas and slippers from Gran. From an Aunt a Grimm book of Fairy Tales, and some socks and underpants that wouldn't fit me for at least five years. Besides those more peaceful gifts, my room looked like the den of a junior terrorist. I had a rifle, two six shooters with holsters, a rocket launcher, a James Bond Beretta standard MI5 issue with concealable shoulder holster, a Crossbow with arrows, and enough caps for all my guns to delay the siege at the Alamo for months.

By comparison, my Dad on the other hand, had seen real action. At nineteen years old he was driving a tank in France. I remember on the odd occasion I could get him to talk about it, he would become very serious and withdrawn. He had a very sad look in his eyes and would always say, "Pray to God, son, it never happens again in your lifetime. It's not something you would ever want to see, ever."

It would be pretty unlikely to happen though, had any threatening foreign power seen my arsenal of weapons on Christmas Day morning, they'd have run a mile. Armed to the teeth, and having shot everything upstairs that deserved it, I made my way down for breakfast. Scrambled eggs and bacon again. It was Mum's attempt to line my stomach with normality before the onslaught that only Christmas Day can bring. As a special treat, she would put grated cheddar cheese in the scrambled eggs. God, it was good, on a thick slice of toast smothered with HP sauce (The scrambled eggs, not the toast!).

"Shall we put the carol concert from King's College on while we have breakfast?" Mum asked as she turned the telly on.

"You can Mum, I'm going to stay in my pyjamas for now, if that's okay?"

"Oh, very funny, monkey, you'll get no breakfast at all if there's any more of your cheek."

I would rather rub broken glass in my eyes than watch the carols Mum, to be honest, I thought. Especially when there were poor quality cartoons on the other side. This was the 60's, there were three channels to make your selection from. It was the only time I can remember when anything involving the church on telly was permitted. I could tolerate about four or five good old traditional favourites before turning over to Tom and Jerry while Mum was in the kitchen. There was always a healthy helping of gratuitous cartoon violence. What would Christmas Day be without it?

"What happened to the carol service?" Mum would ask suspiciously on re-entering the living room.

"It's half time, Mum, so I just put Tom and Jerry on for a minute."

"I'll give you half time, they were lovely those Christmas carols."

"Yeah, but Tom has just been smashed full in the face with a clothes iron, and all his teeth have fallen out one at a time leaving him with a hilarious toothless grin."

No answer, just a frown and shake of the head.

"I'll sing some carols for you later Mum, if you like?"

"No, it's okay, you watch your Tom and Jerry, we don't

want Judy getting upset and howling."

Charming! I had the voice of an angel. The Headmaster at St. Johns Primary School held choirboy auditions, and after one verse of 'All Things Bright and Beautiful', I was in. The Headmaster was called Mr. Brewer. Quite a stern man, but he had humour in him and went to watch Blackpool F.C. so he couldn't be all that bad. He had a presence that improved child behaviour instantly when he appeared. There was no messing about when Mr. Brewer walked into class. He was tough but fair. A nice guy who wanted you to enjoy school and do well. I wasn't allowed to join the choir at St. Johns as it was a Church of England School and we were Protestant Methodists. I don't remember signing up to be a P.M. but that's what Mum and Dad said, so I went along with it. My Dad gave me much more logical reasons not to be in the choir than any religion ever could. It would mean working at weddings on Saturdays so I would miss Blackpool games. I declined my invite to join the choir on religious grounds.

Mr. Brewer saw Dad and me at Blackpool's next home game and smiled and nodded knowingly. I smiled back weakly through my lying eyes, and felt that I may have plummeted down Mr. Brewer's list of respected pupils.

After breakfast I adapted the 'Christmas Eve' song to, the 'Christmas Day' song, and although my excitement levels had dropped considerably after present opening, I was still rattling off some beauties. "It's Christmas Day, It's Christmas Day, some work for nought, some work for pay"... "Take out your skis, prepare your sleigh"... "Fear not your fears, nor your dismay"... "Hip hip, hip hip, hip hip, hooray." The more serious rhymes always took on a Dickensian type of language to incorporate the desperate misery angle of that era. The dafter and more meaningless the lyrics, the giddier I got. "Beseech thy love, for sooth to say" and then hide my head under a cushion for ten minutes until the spirit of Dickens had left the building. If the final ridiculous line was just crazy but rhymed, it had the ability to nearly make me sick with joyous excitement at my own unbridled silliness. Usually followed by a burp of satsuma, chocolate and partially digested scrambled eggs and bacon (with cheese and HP sauce).

That is what Christmas did though. It just made you so happy and content to have all your presents and a tree to squint at and a huge dinner to look forward to. I did however, always struggle with what lay beyond the joys of the Christmas holidays though. That dreaded date when all of the merriment was taken down and boxed away for another twelve months. A return to school, where all things serious took place. A place that even as a five year old I would worry about. How come everyone else seemed to understand things that I didn't? No one looked worried or bothered by anything. Was I the only kid who couldn't wait for the clock to hit three forty p.m. so I could get back to my own cosy little world at home? I worried about everything. Reading, writing, tying my shoes, tying my tie, French lessons, maths, girls (yes, even at five!), football, cricket, teachers I found attractive (yes, even at five!).

I bet Hawking was just the same at my age. He had probably managed to tie his shoes and tie by then though, and moved on to singularities and string theories. I did try to imagine the Universe being infinite once. I went cross eyed, passed out, and had a banging headache for a week. It has seemed at times that he and I were linked in some mysterious way. He was a genius who dedicated his life and incredible mind to the discovery of some of the secrets of the Universe... and I'm bonkers. Almost as if I am the dark matter that he has been searching for all his life.

Mum ended up in a residential home for eighteen months before she was admitted to hospital for her final weeks. It very sadly meant that she would spend her last Christmas away from all those wonderful memories that we all had at home. I went to visit her in the afternoon on Christmas Day as there was a party for the residents and relatives at the home. I don't think she even realised what day it was. There were entertainers and musicians on and it broke my heart to sit and watch her looking confused and then smiling at me when our eyes met. I think I was more in need of help at this point, than Mum. You always feel that you should have done more, and been with them much longer and more often than you were. She would introduce me as her husband sometimes to the other residents. I'm not sure what their expressions said. Staff members would smile and say,

"This is David, Peggy, he's your son, is what you mean?"

"I know who he is" she would say, smiling at me.

You sure did Mum, you sure did.

9. STUPID SCHOOL (I WON'T NOT LEARN NOTHING)

Whenever I was out and about with Mum, we would bump into other women she knew. Their main concern was when I was starting school. (Don't keep reminding her you silly mare, I might get to be eight or nine before they realise!)

"Oh, he starts this September. We got him in at St. Johns on Church Street. His Sister goes there, so she can keep an eye on him."

"Aw, I'm sure he'll be fine. Are you looking forward to starting school David?"

Oh yeah, can't wait. What do you think? I would think to myself before saying, "Yes thank you, and thank you for asking. I'm going to be in Mrs. Moseley's class at St. Johns."

I had no idea who Mrs. Moseley was, but had been reassured she was a really nice lady. Very kind and fun. She loved reading stories to children. As long as attending school simply entailed me sitting daydreaming and not being asked to do anything, then I would consider attending. But I began to suspect there was a ruse to all the descriptions of this lovely fun place, where pressure, tests and maths were a rarity. I had hoped colouring and playing in the sand pit formed the bulk of the curriculum. It sounded too good to be true. It was.

I was a very brave boy that first morning at school. Once I had been prised off the back garden gate, and had my teeth crow barred from the front door frame, the rest of the journey was tantrum free, due to the fact that there was no oxygen in the boot of the car. To tell the truth, Mum took me on the tram. This was Blackpool in 1964. People still went paddling with their trouser legs rolled up and a knotted hanky on their heads. Traditionally, the holidaymakers were folks from inland factory towns, where no one could afford shoes, so people just dipped their feet in hot tar and laced their toes up instead. They worked twenty three hours a day, for half a penny a month. The one hour they were allowed off, they had to sit in a barrel of cold water while slightly more wealthy people punched them in the face. The Sixties in the North West was no place for softies.

Fresh off the tram, and trying to look tough and cool by not holding Mum's hand, we wandered in through the school gates with other terrified looking five-year olds being dragged in by the hair. This was mildly reassuring, as some were clearly more traumatised than me at the prospect of starting school. There's always someone dafter and worse off than yourself, my Mum would say cheerily when I was down in the dumps.

There must have been thirty or so gormless looking youngsters clinging on to their parents in the school yard. All waiting for the process of enlightenment to begin. Eventually, with the need to pee or be sick, or both, reaching epidemic levels, we were rounded up and torn roughly from our loved ones by Miss Moseley. Miss Moseley, was only slightly larger than any of us. She did have a very smiley, kind and welcoming nature, which eased my sick feeling a bit. Much of what happened next is very much a blur. Not just that day, to be honest, but the entirety of my school days.

"Hello, its David isn't it? Come on in and find yourself somewhere to sit."

Miss Moseley seemed to know me and she knew my

Mum too by the way she was smiling and chatting.

Hey this seems to be okay so far. This Miss Moseley character seems like a really nice lady.

There was lots of waving and kisses been blown by teary eyed grown-ups at this point. They all swore they would return later in the day for collection. I have to report that some kids fell apart completely at this stage, and took a good twenty minutes to compose themselves again. Miss Moseley did her best to get everyone calmed down and sat where they were happy. I am pretty certain my first hand up question was, "Miss Moseley, what time is break at please?" In my defence, it was because my bladder was painfully full. Surviving for an hour and a half would be tricky.

I interrupt the writing of this strange little tale for the following New Year TV bombshell announcement. It is New Year's Day 2018, and the BBC has just shown an advert proudly announcing that tonight, they will air a programme entitled 'Sue Perkins and the Chimp Sanctuary'. That's the last penny they ever get off me, even though, as a bonkers cheeky monkey, I may well end up at Sue's hostel for run down chimps. Oh and while I'm at it, I also watched the movie 'Spectre' recently! What a crock of nonsense. The Broccoli bunch need to sit down and watch 'Live and Let Die' over and over and over again until they remember how to make a Bond film that has a story and action sequences that are at least, barely believable. I would think the main problem for the actors in 'Spectre', was not convulsing with laughter at what they were being asked to do and say. I also caught some snippets of the Pope's Christmas speech the other day and he was saying, what is wrong with people now? Loud, rude, stupid, bad mannered, always looking at a mobile phone.

Apart from that he seems like quite a nice bloke.

Back to Mr. Pee-Pants and the enormous wait till playtime.

"Yes, it's David isn't it?"

"Yes, Miss."

"Do you need the toilet, David? Is that why you're asking?"

"Yes, Miss."

"Right, well off you pop, you know where the toilets are in the cloakroom don't you?"

"Yes, Miss."

Five other hands shoot up as I push my little seat back and it scrapes a squeal on the wooden floor.

"Alright, alright, some of you can wait until break time I'm sure. When David comes back, someone else can go. Off you go David, chop, chop."

"Yes Miss Moseley, thank you, Miss."

I strolled leisurely out to the sanctuary of the cloakroom and the loo. Suckers, I thought to myself, as I wandered around the cloakroom a bit, sizing up everyone's coats, just observing how rich or poor everyone else was. I had an 'I'm in no hurry thank you very much' piddle in the toilets, and then zig-zagged my way back to the classroom taking as long as possible. As soon as I got back in the room there were a dozen more hands up waving for attention.

"Alright, alright, put your hands down thank you, you can't all be needing the toilet. Did you find it okay, David? You were gone quite a while."

"Yes Miss, sorry Miss."

I have no idea what we did for the next hour or so. All I could think of was playtime and kicking a ball around for ten minutes in the school yard. That was if you were allowed by the bigger kids who ran the games and picked the sides. We were little league. The big boys played in the main rectangle with a size five football. We were in the small playground with a smaller ball, so we wouldn't get knocked over, crushed and killed. For the Sixties, that was cutting edge health and safety in action. It meant we had to play around girls who were skipping! Some were even more disturbed than that. They were running around making neighing sounds atop invisible horses. Clicking their mouths and holding reins that didn't exist. They appeared to be jumping over nothing, in a bid to secure an invisible rosette. Did they really have to gallop and neigh right where the halfway line was? I could see, even at the age of five that females were going to be trouble.

If you tried to shoo them, or boot the ball at their heads accidently, they would herd, and form a stampede of furious pretend showjumpers slapping their thighs and charging straight at you. I'll swear one of them lashed my cheek with an imaginary crop as she sped past. No wonder men are attracted to jodhpur-wearing horsey types.

But these enraged horsey girls were not to be trifled with. I may well have had more than one slapped face after my wayward accidental shooting had drifted their way during break times. In addition to getting my face slapped regularly by make believe showjumpers, another interaction with womanhood came in the form of Emma Peel. I was watching the very entertaining and addictive 'The Avengers' every week on TV. Mrs. Peel was the gorgeous sexily clad female agent who beat the holy crap out of baddies every episode. Now I'm no expert in the field of what happens when and why, but I defy any young man to watch Emma Peel in 'The Avengers' and not get some awkward discomfort in his underpants. Trying to watch an episode with my Mum, Dad and Sister on a Saturday evening, was no push over. Especially if I had bathed, and was ready for bed as soon as it finished, in my pyjamas. I had to try and sit nonchalantly, with my hands discreetly between my legs. Mum was surprised when I would happily sprint up to bed as soon as it finished. A quick peck goodnight on the cheek for all, then still with my hand on woody via the pockets in my dressing gown, I was up to the safety of my bedroom for some quiet moments alone with Emma Peel.

My attraction to the opposite sex, formed at an alarmingly early age.

Back to the giggling, galloping, lunatics on invisible horses. We held a mid- playground conference and persuaded the equestrians to keep their show-jumping escapades to the perimeter of the junior play area. This would keep ball to face injuries down to a minimum, and prevent the interruption of imaginary world cup games. I still got a slap every time certain riders went past. I had actually told one unlucky young lady that she was my girlfriend, and when we were grown up I would marry her. The mechanics of her being my girlfriend were limited to me looking at her sometimes. It worked well for both parties. They tell their mates they've got a boyfriend too, then ignore you completely and refuse to look at you. When you do dare to go anywhere near them, they turn beetroot red, start giggling, merge into the centre of their pack of friends so you can't see them, and keep shouting 'Go away'.

I have had quite a number of relationships that have involved more than this, and can report that they were complicated, painful, and usually ended up in heartbreak and tears. For me. I will throw this lovely little conundrum in at this point. Does every one find, that anybody they really like, they don't fancy, and anyone that they really fancy, they don't like? What kind of a dirty trick is that for the Universe to play? Hey, Hawking? How about asking the big fella to shed some light on that for a problem? Never mind about Higgs Boson for Christ's sake, get some theories jotted down for finding a member of the opposite sex who you like and want to jump on a dozen times a day. Or rather, I should say, share tender romantic and intimate loving moments with.

So my first year at Primary School was filled mostly with looking forward to break times, playing football, getting slapped by girls, and daydreaming about sexual fantasies. Just your regular five year old really. There are certain things that are guaranteed to embarrass any young child in front of elders or parents. One in particular is anything romantic or sexual. You know the sort of thing. Watching a movie where there is imminent kissing about to begin, and you slowly disappear into a crouching format with your knees bent and your legs up in front of your face with support from the elbows to protect any side view intrusion as well. You hope it will be a short peck rather than a long slurp sloppy affair lasting for ten minutes or more.

The only time my Mum ever said anything to me about matters of a sexual nature, was when she discovered a piece of paper that I had typed a rude little fantasy on. Seeing the words typed out on paper somehow gave them much greater power. I was mortified that she had found it, but she just said, "Just be careful what you write young man, please... okay?" I nodded with my bright red face, and looking at the floor said, "Yeah okay, will do, sorry Mum." She ruffled my hair. I was ten.

10. MATHEMATICAL CONFUSIONS

That first year at school was just all mucking about really. A bit of reading, some quality time in the sand pit, a lot of quiet time with head down on folded arms on your desk lid. Nothing too worrying or taxing. I had seen year two teacher Mrs. Williams. She looked a good deal sterner, and I had heard she was keen on maths and picking you out to read aloud in class. I felt sick at the prospect, even before we broke up for the summer holidays. When we came back in September, I would be faced with adding, subtracting, dividing, and times-ing. What? Could *you* spell multiplication at six? (Not you, Hawking! You probably worked out how far it was from the womb to the stage door, and had calculated the precise angle of trajectory to ensure safe passage out into the next dimension. No calculator required.)

One of my stand out memories from very early on at St. Johns, was the first Christmas Fair. All the classrooms had been done up with decorations. Ours had a huge tree covered in ornaments that were for sale. The proceeds went to charity and the teachers' night out. There were stalls as well, selling second hand books and toys. It was lovely wandering in and out of the other classrooms looking for things at bargain prices. I remember persuading Mum to buy me some hard back annuals that looked really good, and a little model Spitfire for killing Germans and blowing up U-Boats in the bath. The Spitfire would provide wonderful air cover for my frogmen, free with soap powder if my memory serves me right? They were modelled on 'Thunderball', the Bond movie. The frogmen would take cover in huge mounds of Matey suds, and then pop up to reveal U-Boat locations. The Spitfire would do the rest. Swooping down time after time and blowing the filthy Nazis clean out of the water. I slept well as a child. That would be after a good old bedtime read of my Rupert the Bear annual, whose gentle poetic humour would calm me down after the horrors of war in the bath tub. It was a great Christmas Fair. All the teachers were in their own clothes, and smiling a lot more than usual. Clothes that demonstrated their limited knowledge of fashion. The smiling, may well have been Gin related.

They all seemed to know and like my Mum a lot. Some would even call her Peggy, which made me feel like I could probably get away with just about anything at school.

"How is he getting on? I hope he's not causing you any bother?" My Mum quizzed Mrs. Marsh, who I quite fancied because she wore all black like Emma Peel.

"He's doing fine, he's a good lad, most of the time."

It was a good job the reply came with a cheeky smile and eye contact. I'm sure I'd been told off a number of times by her for kicking the ball too hard in the general direction of club equine. Perhaps she preferred football to show jumping too? My final purchase at the fair, before we went to get the 26 bus home, was a little Santa Claus sitting on a swing on the big Christmas tree. He was made of bright red and white felt, with black mittens, belt and boots. He had a big friendly smile and I thought it would look fantastic on our tree. He did have a disproportionately large head compared to the rest of his body which was a touch disconcerting. I satisfied myself with the idea that it was extra storage room for children's addresses. You need a whopper of a skull to remember where everyone lives on planet earth. Especially if you're driving in the dark with just the red hooter of a reindeer for guidance. It was the only decoration I was ever given sole charge of. I was even allowed to pick a spot on the tree where it could go. The fact that it wasn't breakable, sealed it.

I used to put him right at the front, about half way up. I would pull a tree light and position it just above his large head. From there, he could see up the fairy's skirt if he was bored, and straight across from him, was the nativity scene and his best mate, 'The little baby Jesus'. I have no idea where my little Santa is now. In heaven I guess, with Jesus and God, smiling down on us knowingly.

So Infants' Year One, was negotiated without too much distress or drama. Year two was going to prove a whole lot trickier. The very word Maths still makes me feel sick to the stomach. It was this second year when we were introduced to it in a practical sense. It didn't make sense to me at all, practical or otherwise. What I'm getting at, is that we were obliged to actually try and work out problems with pen and paper, as opposed to using a crayon to draw over the numbers one to nine on a printed sheet with a colour of your own choice. This was to get you used to writing numbers free-hand, all by yourself. My request to return to Miss Moseley's class to enjoy colouring instead of thinking was refused, despite my demand for the issue to be taken to the Attorney General. I could have got this from watching too much of 'A Man Called Ironside', a TV crime drama about a paraplegic busy-body American copper played by Raymond Burr.

Mrs. Williams was not at all impressed if she picked on you without warning to give an answer to a question and you just stared blankly into space open mouthed. She suddenly requested my opinion on eleven minus four. Never an easy one for me. If you made a complete dog's dinner of it and came up with something as crazy as, two, you would be treated to further interrogation.

"Don't be silly, David, how have you got that as your answer? Think, and try again."

I couldn't understand how she had even seen me, hiding under my desk with my blazer over my head.

"Come out from under your desk David and stop acting daft. You know you can do it, you just don't try hard enough, now think."

I would emerge from under my blazer with my mouth shut and a serious thinking expression on my face hoping for some kind of a miracle to occur. Would the answer drop into my grey swirling mist of a brain and save the day? Think Hogie think for Christ's sake. Eleven? Eleven? What is eleven when it's at home? Okay wait, one off eleven is ten, yep, ten, and then four more off ten? Not four you dick head, you've already taken one off a second ago. Oh yeah, right, so what's one off four? Okay, okay, three, so eleven minus three is? Not eleven, ten you idiot, ten, ten minus three you stupid bird brain. Oh yeah, ten minus three is….. When I finally look up, the classroom is empty except for me. Mrs. Williams is half way home in her grey Morris Minor, and my classmates are tucking into a Club biscuit and some Angel Delight in the kitchen at their Nan's.

"Ssss, Ssss Seven?"

"Finally! Really David, I'm surprised at you. You need to pay a little bit more attention in class young man and less time daydreaming about football."

"Yes, Mrs. Williams, sorry Mrs. Williams."

Maths psycho.

For your information, I was daydreaming about Emma Peel in a black cat suit. In fairness, she was playing up front for Brazil, had just scored a hat-trick, and celebrated by knocking the goalie out with a karate chop on the way back to the centre circle.

Maths was, and still is, just an inconvenient requirement as far as I'm concerned. For those of you who try to convince me otherwise, save your breath. That includes you Hawking (God rest your soul). Do you think that Russell Grant sits at home with a calculator and a log book? (A Logarithms book, not the paperwork history of his current car), trying to work out how much space and time weighs? No of course not. He looks at the Stargazer app on his tablet and then writes down what's going to happen to everyone on the planet that day. Depending on when you were born and at what time, of course. He doesn't even have to write it up on the blackboard to prove anything. He's that good. It just flows through him and out onto the paper. And that, is that. Messages from the Universe regarding pretty much everything. Sometimes, he even gets told what's going to happen for the entire following twelve months. It's also split it into different categories, such as Money, Romance, Health, and Work, for him. How many equations have you got to sort that lot out Mr. Theory of Everything? None, that's how many. Despite all that, I sincerely regret never having had a chance to meet you Mr. Hawking, sir.

I did eventually get the gist of mathematics. It's lots of irritating numbers jumbled up to cheese you off. Don't ever let anyone tell you Mathematics is beautiful. Art is beautiful, nature is beautiful, music is beautiful, and women are beautiful. The Universe is beautiful, maths is puck ugly with the sole purpose of doing your nut in. It also has the ability to have you soil your pants the night before an exam.

As for English, I was terrifyingly picked out to read aloud a few times in class, but rescued myself with the remarkable ability to have a coughing fit, or a nose bleed after only two or three lines of reading. I was surprised no one ever saw, or heard me, punch myself in the face to start the nosebleed. It took quite a whack. Not easy to pull off whilst stalling over the word 'facsimile', which I hilariously pronounced wrongly as 'fascist smile'. I assumed my version of the word referred to a mildly amused Nazi. Why there would even be a word to describe such a thing gives you a little peep into my rat's nest of a brain. I am half wittingly half way to being a full blown halfwit. So much to look forward to.

My tactic of face thumping was a stroke of genius when it came to reading out loud in class. This too could explain why I have never been an avid reader, more of a David reader, to be fair. It was years before I realised I didn't have to punch myself in the face to enjoy a good old read. I was thirty eight before I stopped reading out loud though. There I was, on the bus from O'Connell St Dublin, heading up to the airport. I have got a copy of 'A Brief History of Time' out at arms-length, reading my head off. I was nodding knowingly, yes, like Jesus did regarding my turkey exploits, smiling at every other person on the packed Airport Shuttle Bus. Oh yes, ladies and gentlemen, you heard me right. 'A Brief History of Time'. Read it and weep. I cried at the Introduction. Not because it was emotional, but because I couldn't understand a single word of it. Written in laymen's terms, my arse.

There I was reading aloud loads of mis-pronounced words, smiling and nodding, when a hand the size of a donkey's head appeared on my shoulder.

"Listen here, Einstein, if yer don't feckin' pipe down,

I'll shove yer little book of horoscopes right up your stupid feckin arse yer feckin great eejit."

Which roughly translated for those of you who haven't visited the Emerald Isle is, "I say old chap, is there any chance you might like to enjoy the delights of your novel in a less noisy fashion? It looks a splendid jaunt I must say. However, if you are reluctant to agree to my polite request, I shall be forced to hide your informative purchase deep inside your anal canal."

Some poetic licence has been used to beef things up a bit. His hand was more the size of an Alsatian's head to be honest. Think Hitler and Blondi if you must. What a band that would have been. Don't you be laughing, Hawking? I've said this before, and I'll say it again. People very often confuse Astronomy and Astrology. It's a very easy mistake to make. Astronomers look out into the universe and want to do some sums and spoil it. Astrologists look out into the universe and think... Ooh, that's pretty, I'm going to write some lovely little stories to cheer everyone up.

Mum had a real liking for the horoscopes in the paper. If I was a bit down in the dumps she would say, "Let's have a look at your stars and see what they say." It would always be good news and cheer me up and make me chuckle. I think she made some of it up. She still does.

Located around the same area as the horoscopes was the small crossword which she could do in five minutes flat or less. I still do that same crossword every day. It's where a lot of my messages from her arrive. Sometimes one word that is so relevant it sends shivers down my back, but it's the multiple clues linked together that really freak me out.

I get help from her and my Dad quite regularly if I get

stuck. I can hear them saying, "Go on, what's the clue? How many letters?" Within seconds, I get the answer that I was struggling to find. Funny how asking the old folks for help will, more often than not, point me in the right direction.

11. GOOD GOD, WHAT THE DEVIL?

All this talk of Astronomy and Astrology does get you thinking about the universe and that age old questions 'Why are we here?' 'Is there a God?' 'What happens when we die?' 'Shall I have a curry?' These are all great conundrums for getting that little rice pudding lump of grey matter to reach out and seek the answers to the most puzzling and profound questions. I have spoken with many people who claim they don't give any of these a single moment's thought. Do I believe them? No. Do I have the answers to any of them myself? Yes. (Er, no, not really)

Perhaps you were wondering when I'd come clean. Question No.1 Why are we here? Well if you are of the scientific persuasion, you will have arrived at no other conclusion than we are here thanks to the wonders of Chemistry, Physics and Biology. They all of course invented themselves from nothing, because they can do whatever they want, as they are the laws of nature. Self-appointed laws of nature I might add. They needed no more than a grey swirling mist of primordial nothingness to get cooking. This grey soup originated where exactly? I have no idea, I'm just saying, that's all. It just so happens that a great host of unlit very dark chemicals were hanging around with absolutely nothing to do. They got chatting, sorry, reacting, and one thing led to another. It all became a bit too hot and bothered and… Bang! All hell broke loose. A bit like a night out in Blackpool. Thirteen billion years later, here we are, Planet Earth and Blackpool.

"Not one to be critical, you understand, but there does appear to be some gaps in the evidence here, your Honour."

"Noted, Mr. Hogwart, proceed."

"Yes M'lud, it's Hogwash actually."

"Clearly, Mr. Hogwart... Please proceed."

"Yes your Honour, thank you. It does take us right back to that first dark night in question".

"Batman?"

" Er, no, night with an 'N', m'lud."

"With you, proceed."

"Well I'm sorry to say that the theories just seem to disappear down a big black hole your Honour, and leave the door wide open to any number of complex and soul searching possibilities."

"Are you talking in riddles Mr. Hogwart? None of what you say appears to make any sense."

"Thank you m'lud, it's very kind and wise of you to say so."

It's all just smoke (the grey swirling mist kind) and mirrors (the image and light reflecting kind). But then never be afraid of anything. Imagine life with nothing to fear. You are allowed to fear one thing though... the worst.

Question No.2. Is there a God? Dawkins, leave the room, Hawking, put your angelic little hand down. Let's just say the jury is out on this one. Put another 'O' in God, and what do you get? So there it is, in the blink of an eye he whips his 'O' out and Good is now God. So he was called Good originally, and then changed it to God? Yep. Bit big headed calling yourself Good from the word go isn't it? It sure is, but when you are God, you can do anything you choose, especially if you've been good. And we all know who comes every Christmas Eve if you've been good don't we? That's right... the little baby Jesus. The Almighty needed to sound a bit more in control, and he realised people would have had a right go about him calling himself Good.

Ever noticed what happens to the word Devil if you take the D off? Yep, it's spelt wrong. Have another look. What the!?... Evil? What do you make of that then me old china plate? Devil and Evil, Good and God! What in the name of heaven and hell is going on here? They aren't just coincidences to set minds a-wondering now are they? But are they the mind of God or the mind of man? Well I'm not sure to be honest, but never mind. Have you tried that little trick with your own name? What, David? Yep. I have actually. Apparently I am a tiny green plant eating insect. Not aphid, you idiot, avid. Oh yes of course, how silly of me. Well I can't really say I'm an avid anything. Oh wait, yes I can. An avid day dreamer, even at night.

When your heart sings and your spirit soars for whatever reason, there is a feeling within you that is almost impossible to describe. An empty mind and a still heart are all that you require. I certainly qualify for the first part. Euphoria is as close as we English can muster. 'Joie de vivre' may well be a better description. Damn those French and their romantic expressive language. Whatever you decide to call it, both you and I know it is there. You don't know how, or why, you just know. A feeling of belonging, a strange sense of connection to everything and everyone, man, woman, beast, plant, rock and object.

It's not surprising really. We have all been here together since the planet formed 4.54 billion years ago. I wasn't there to observe this of course, but the particles that make up who I am, and those that make up you, and all things on the planet, were here then as they are here now. Let's just say they've grown up a little. We are all here together, alone. On a journey, caught in a stream that ebbs and flows towards the sea of the universe. Raise your eyes to the heavens, let the universe see your face. Or, if you're too busy, just send a photo by email. The universe will get back to you.

I have just been and splashed my face with cold water and can happily report that I'm feeling much better. You may choose not to believe me, about Planet Earth, not the water splash episode, and you may be right to do so. You may also like to consider that the truth is only something you personally believe in. A choice. There are truths. You just have to pick the ones that matter to you. Whether to let something into your heart and soul or not. If you need more convincing, read a bit of Hawking and Dawkins, regarding the age and nature of our home, not about truth and lies. They aren't so much Morecambe and Wise, as Itchy and Scratchy. Actually Dawkins isn't funny at all. He would have been on The Simpsons if he was. Despite being massively intelligent the pair of them, we are all just papers blowing in the wind and hoping to stumble across an alchemist or the secret of the universe itself. So, is there a God or isn't there? Well, let's just say there is good in everything and leave it at that for now. Now, is all we've got, and all we will ever have. Good God, now there's something or nothing to think about.

Question No.3. What happens when we die? The most popular choices are burial or cremation. But what happens to our soul, our spirit? Well most of it is usually stolen and drunk by the house clearance guys. Or it just gets poured down the sink if it looks a bit old and smelly. Down the plughole and into the streams below that lead out to the sea. The Irish Sea via the sewage pipes at Central Pier.

I have learnt since my Mum passed away, to be much less of a cynic, and to have more faith in things. I have always viewed the spiritual stuff with casual ignorance.

Actually I viewed it with an unhealthy feeling of outsiders' envy. I never thought of myself as spiritual until after Mum died and I went into business with an old school friend of my Sister's.

Kath is very spiritual. She does readings for people who come back to see her time after time. I used to sit and listen to her talking with her spiritual friends and think, what a load of groin fruit. One thing I have always felt I did have, was very good intuition and instinct. Gut feeling. Sometimes something more. Being a rational doubting Thomas though, I always believed that my intuition and instinct was nothing more than logical realism. I could just work out certain things by being sensible and applying common sense to experiences that seemed unusual.

There have been many incidents over the last ten years of a nature that this cynical doubting Thomas of a man has found difficult to explain and impossible to ignore.

The luckiest thing that will ever happen to you, is that you exist. Better splash my face again I think. Make the most of it (not splashing my face, existing).

I am only just beginning to realise that I feel as if I'm being watched over. Community Support Officers, CCTV cameras, and Mum. I started to change after the death of my Mum. I was drawn to a number of tracks and found myself listening to them more intently than usual. One track in particular called, rather appropriately, 'It's your world now'. It is a beautiful track, and reduces me to tears every time I play it. It makes me think fondly of my Mum, and feel that she is connecting with me through the music and lyrics. There is a line that I knew was meant to alter me as a person. I needed a lift. Times were difficult. I had sunk to becoming someone who was unhappy and discontent with everything. Including myself. The line that stood out to me every single play was, 'Be part of something good, leave something good behind' I took it as a very personal message to me.

It felt like my Mum was really upset that I was disillusioned with life. Turning into an angry man who had lost interest even in music, laughing, and being silly. This little sign, was not a one off. There have been very many over the last few years. Whenever they have occurred, my instinct has been to sit up and take note. It has been quite overwhelming at times. I feel it is coming directly from my Mum or maybe from an older friend, the soul of the Universe.

The pain and loneliness of losing my Mum began to change me quite dramatically as a person. At first I was certain the book was a debt of gratitude to my parents for doing their very best for my sister and me while they were here. As the process has unfolded though, I have started to think it's actually about writing, itself. Writing was one of the things I enjoyed at school. An omen that I may have failed to notice during an English lesson, was a comment made by a very strict teacher at secondary school.

His comments about you and the work you produced were best avoided if at all possible. Mr. (Piggy) Bradshaw, verbally destroyed nearly every piece of homework he was handing back to my classmates. He stood at the front of the class with a pile of exercise books in front of him. He would pick each one up individually and flick to the page for a quick reminder of what he had suffered and marked. He didn't say a word until closing the book, and then peering over his specs he would bark a name. The owner of the surname would raise a nervous hand to locate themselves on his radar. His look would say a great deal, but for the really unlucky ones he would accompany his disgusted expression with such helpful comments as, "Idiot", "Garbage", "Pathetic", "Imbecile". Piggy was a man of few words, but they were always cutting and hurtfully succinct. A practice strangely frowned upon now in the world of education.

He was well into the aitches, and I was next batsman in. I sat there with my sphincter tightened, ready to be insulted on a spectacular one word scale.

"Hogarth?"

There was a pause as he looked at the page my mindless drivel was scrawled upon. More pause. Oh for God's sake, I'm never going to live this down, I thought as the tension reached small flatulence levels.

"At least you can string sentences together, lad."

It was like I had just been awarded the Nobel Prize for literature, aged twelve.

The relaxation in the anus area caused a short audible blast that spoilt the moment, but the esteem of not being insulted by Piggy Bradshaw was almost orgasmic. My arms got a right pounding at break time, which was a well-known mark of respect back in those days for outstanding achievement. Today, it's called bullying. It's a shame the moment passed me by as sheer relief, rather than an encouraging pointer towards something I might like to take advantage of when leaving school.

Considering it was a decent Grammar School, it was disappointing there wasn't much in the way of career advice and guidance. None of my teachers shared my optimistic ambitions regarding me being Captain of England's Football and Cricket teams. These people were clearly no mugs.

When my writing adventure began, I kept getting drawn to certain bits of information, clips, photos, songs, all sorts. As if by magic or completely out of the blue, they all seemed to be connected and relevant to me and what I was embarking on. Like I had suddenly and unwittingly stepped onto something that was there specifically for me. It felt as if I had finally tuned in to the station I was supposed to be listening to.

One time, I woke up in the middle of the night and wrote a poem. As I awoke, the words were already being spoken in my head, and I quickly sat up and put my lamp on and grabbed my notebook and pen. It came to me in three separate parts. There were no breaks in the words that were coming, and it was as if I wasn't thinking them at all, they were just filing themselves into my inbox. It was quite a disturbing experience, if I'm honest.

It is about a very deep fear that I think we all have. Self-doubt. To me though it was a clue, a signpost, and an answer that I needed to hear. This experience was so strange I shall never forget it, ever.

'No Doubt'

Alone I hear a whispered voice, that taunts and draws me out,

It tempts me to believe and dream, then tortures me with doubt,

It guides my hand and feeds my mind, to lessen my mistakes,

Then walks away with smirking face, a broken man it makes,

It visits when I least expect, an uninvited guest,

Arriving just in time to spoil, a chance to be my best,

Who would invite this loser in, to mock and critique me?

And then I recognise the voice, it's me, it's me, it's me

So do I let this darkness in, or do I stand and fight,

A chance to reinvent myself, and head towards the light,

Have I the time to reignite and see my spirit fly,
Or do I simply fade away, and never even try,
On turning tide with faith and hope, I rise to tell my tale,
And bless the breeze that bares no ill that gently fills my sail,
This doubt I have is all of me, this doubt I have is mine,
No doubt that it belongs to me, to stop me rise and shine,
A doubt I never welcomed here, it hides where I can't see,
It lies within the soul of me, and never lets me be.

Of all the songs that resonated with me as a child, it was always the tunes and not the words that I took most pleasure and interest in. Melody, harmony and rhythm always stirred my emotions. Three lovely girls. Changes in chords, harmonies and melodies that would resonate deeply, as if their very existence was woven into my soul. Maybe they are. Perhaps sound waves and their vibrations are part of our living fabric. A kind of sound tapestry that we're all receiving. Put the right combination out there and the emotions have no choice but to respond.

I heard a very curious audio post a while ago that included a recording of swarming locust sounds. It was slowed down on the recording many times to reveal something quite astonishing. They were singing 'When you wish upon a Star' from Pinocchio. My first musical memories were of songs that featured in Disney cartoons. Mum was just as keen to go and see these films as Kate and I were. 'When you wish upon a star', was the first song I can recall that made the hairs on the back of my neck stand up. The lyrics carry more weight and meaning than any little song in a cartoon for kids should have the right to do. Second on this list is, 'If I were a rich man'. I played it over and over to the point of my Mum commenting, "I think we've heard it enough now David thanks, put something else on, there's a good lad." This was the early days of my record collection. I am guessing my total number of other choices at this point, was two, maybe three, if you count my Jungle Book LP. I had 'Sleepy Joe' by Herman's Hermits and 'Alternate Title' by The Monkees. The original title for the song was 'Randy Scouse Git'. Bit harsh. Sleepy Joe was a wakeup call for me, but as I was only nine when it was released, it may as well have been called Dozy Dave. The Topol song 'If I were a rich man', has a last line I really love. 'Lord who made the Lion and the Lamb, You decreed I should be what I am, would it spoil some vast eternal plan, if, I were a wealthy man?' Well in answer to the last two lines, apparently, yes. I may well have reached that point at last though, where finally you sit up and take notice of all the things that you should, and that make you feel different.

Little things start to happen. More and more helpful signs, pointers, and omens appear to nudge you a bit this way and a little bit that way. Some things begin to mean more than they used to, and you realise it's getting closer and closer to win or bust time. They were always there, I just didn't look. Am I sad? You bet. I don't think I was meant to notice all this stuff until now though. Time marches on, the clock is ticking. I've been skating on very thin ice for many years, but the Universe has never allowed me to fall through completely. Maybe it didn't give up on me because I hadn't yet served my purpose. Whatever that may yet turn out to be?

I had a dream recently that I was walking along a country lane, in very calm warm sunshine. To my right were fields with tall golden stems. A sea of waving strands with little, or no, obvious features.

"Do you see the sunflowers David?" a voice asked quietly and kindly. There were no sunflowers, just stems, thousands and thousands of stems.

"There are no flowers," I said, "only stems."

"Turn around and look again," the voice suggested.

When I turned around, there was a mass of golden sunflowers, thousands of full blooms standing tall with their heads tilting proudly towards the sun.

"If you walk with your head bowed, you will see only shadow. Raise your eyes to the heavens, let the universe see your face." That was it. Crystal clear. A dream I will never forget, ever. It was so lovely and vivid and special that it woke me up. Then I had a pee and went back to sleep. In hindsight, I should have gone to the bathroom really.

"Oh David! Can't you just be serious for once? Just for one minute? You always have to go and spoil it by being silly."

"Sorry Mum, I'm trying."

"Oh you're trying alright!"

"Can I put my Jungle Book LP on then?"

"Yes, go on then, but don't have it on too loud, okay?"

"Okay, cheers Mum.".......

"DAVID! Turn that thing down a bit... what did I tell you?"

Sorry Mum. I hear you, loud and clear.

12. EAST FIFE, FOUR – FORFAR, FIVE

Now which year was I at in school? Oh, that's right, next up was Mrs. Marsh, year three. Tall, slim, redhead. No hair, just a red head. Imposing, smelt nice. She was quite fierce really, but fair. I must have had a few telling offs from her I think. Mainly maths, football, and predominately, for being an idiot.

I remember one time sitting at a group table full of other class gigglers who weren't paying attention either. She sprang on us like a big black panther with a red head. She asked each one of us in turn to explain the answers that we had given to a sum. We all had different sized coloured wooden rods with numerical values to help demonstrate the outcome. My attempt resembled the remains of a Caribbean beach shack that had been destroyed by a hurricane. The accompanying comments to my rod display included non- mathematical terms like, football, Emma Peel, Stingray and Jiminy Cricket. The other po-faced children at our table wore expressions of sympathetic bewilderment at my lack of mathematical prowess. It was mingled however, with a smiling approval of just how nutty my answer was in trying to bamboozle Mrs. Marsh. I received an open handed slap to the side of my head for coming up with such insolent nonsense. My ear was ringing for the rest of the day. But being tough, I refused to answer it. I may even have gone to bed early that night.

It was about this time that I started to pal around with one or two other lads who were footy and girl focused. Dave Williams and John Walker were funny, and loved music too. It made perfect sense. In addition, Dave was hard as nails, and John was the focus for every love sick girl at our school. Even some of the big girls. I had myself a minder and a kitty magnet as my pals. I was gutted a couple of years later when we were separated as team captains for football. It would mean rivalry among mates on the pitch.

Dave was one of those young lads you encounter every now and then that seems to be way older than his years. He was a bigger build than us all, and much brighter too. Good at maths, and always near, or at the top of the class. My highest rank was sixth or seventh. When it was coming up to eleven plus time, I slipped to somewhere around fourteen or fifteen in the pop pickers chart. Mrs. Crawford gave me a severe pep talk. She told me that if I didn't pull my socks up and got back into the top ten in class, that I would probably fail my eleven plus. I passed my eleven plus daydreaming about being tenth on Mrs. C's list of schoolboys she cared about. After Mrs. Crawford's class, it would be into the last year at junior school with the much feared Mr. Partington. If I got my mind-addled act together in time, I would be off to Grammar School.

That final year in the juniors, we got to play football on proper grass pitches for the first time. We were herded on to a bus on Friday afternoons and driven to a local park that had junior sized pitches. Curiously, they had full sized posts and crossbars that made scoring goals unchallenging to say the least. Whatever size of child happened to be ear marked for goalkeeping duty made no difference whatsoever. This resulted in some wonderful full time scores like 29-13. My maths perked up when it came to football scores. I would go home on Fridays and talk my Mum enthusiastically through each of my seventeen goals in fine 'Match of the Day' detail. I was normally cut short around goal number six to be told to go and run a bath and get cleaned up.

"Bath," she would repeat, interrupting my tale. "You can tell me all about them later when you've had your tea."

I would usually forget later. I have a feeling that is what she hoped would happen. Six goals is enough for any Mum, even for one as kind, lovely, and patient as mine. When I took my tracksuit bottoms off, I would usually be ordered into the back yard to dislodge as much of Grange Park's soil off as possible, rather than leaving it in the bath once the water had drained. Clearing my own mess up was not one of my finer qualities. I would lie there soaking in a lovely hot bath, with Matey suds up to my cheeks. I would re-run in my mind the afternoon's goal scoring heroics. Some of the goals required you to dribble round the less interested and unskilled defenders more than once to make the whole effort seem more worthwhile. Once you got tired of nut-megging and drag-backing these bemused daydreamers, you proceeded towards goal and prepared to break the imaginary net with a rocket of a shot. Real posts, no net, what a bummer. As you neared the goals unchallenged, with a trail of dizzy non athletes in your wake, the task of finishing was a doddle. The image that greeted you resembled that of the smallest mouse you have ever seen, standing terrified in the middle of the entrance to the world's largest aircraft hangar. Unless you now kicked the ground and broke your foot, sending the ball dribbling at snail's pace into the mouse's shins, glory was all yours. Whack! Ball fizzes past ducking mouse with its eyes closed and hands protecting its face. Yes! 13-6 I shouted, as wheeling away my delighted team mates would pat me on the back and ruffle my hair in celebration. Meanwhile the tiny mouse, relieved that the shot didn't hit him full in the face and kill him, scampers seventy yards (20 yards at most) to collect the un-netted thunderbolt.

"How many is that you've got now, Hogie?"

"Err, seven I think?" More hair ruffles.

"How long is left, Sir?"

"Ten minutes." Mr. Partington admits, smiling weakly at the mouse.

"Ten minutes? Right come on lads, we could get fifty if we keep going at this rate."

It was my duty as team Captain, to ensure we destroyed our opponents mentally as well as physically for our own squad morale.

You could barely hear yourself think on the bus back to school. Some of the greatest goals ever to be scored in the history of Junior Football were argued over by exaggerating ten year olds.

"David?! Thunderbirds is on in five minutes and tea is nearly ready. I think you've been in that bath quite long enough." Mum would shout up the stairs.

I would jump out of the bath, get dried and dressed and be down for quality teatime TV and my Mums awesome cooking before you could say 'Don't bother with a quick sausage shuffle now Davey boy, save it for later, after your tea, some telly, and when you've had a nice little read of your Avengers annual at bedtime'. Done, and done.

It may not even have been 'Thunderbirds' that night. It could have been 'Banana Splits' (one banana, two banana, three banana, four) or 'Stingray' (they're gaining on us, Troy) or 'Supercar' (gee Mitch, it's getting awful dark) or 'Fireball XL5' (on our way home) or 'Joe 90' (rubbish) or 'Captain Scarlett' (ditto). Gerry, Gerry, Gerry, where did it all go wrong my friend? You did redeem yourself with 'UFO' though. I'll give you that sunshine. I don't recall exactly when they were on, but they were absolutely awesome, bordering on dreadful. Such a heady mix.

What really mattered was, when they were on, anything could happen in the next half hour. Being a big fan of the Gerry Anderson teatime puppetry shows, I asked for, and got, a 'Stingray' toy for my fifth birthday. I think I wet myself with excitement. It was a big plastic replica model with all the right looks, fins, missile ports etc. To say that it didn't do much though is justifiably accurate. It had a cable attached to where its anus would have been on the underside, which in turn led to a huge grey remote control device. Not remote at all, as it was attached, and the farthest you were ever away from Stingray, was about three feet. It had motorised wheels for forward motion, and the propeller at the back end of the vessel lit up and spun. That was it. After electrocuting myself mildly with it in the bath, the huge Ever Ready batteries were removed for my own safety. I was left with a toy that had an eerie looking umbilical cord trailing behind it. Dangling even more scarily at the end, was what looked like, a dead baby grey whale.

I did the honourable thing, and severed the corpse from the mother whale. I was rewarded with a clip round the ear for taking the law into my own hands.

"I'll box your ears David, if you ever take the scissors to your toys again."

"Why? Are you sending my ears off in the post somewhere?"

More ear boxing for my cheek. Stingray did look better though, now the unsightly umbilical cord and trailing corpse had been removed. It sat on my drawer tops nice and flush, free from the heartache of it's still-born offspring.

Mum was no easy touch when it came to getting things that I wanted, but she seemed to manage to cobble together enough to buy me what I had asked for eventually. She didn't have a job, she was a stay at home Mum who kept the house spotless, and loved cooking, washing and ironing. She worked before she and my Dad met. They were in their late twenties when they married and had Kate and me, and luckily Dad earned enough for Mum not to need a job too. She would squirrel away bits of her housekeeping money to buy things for us on a regular basis. I don't know how she managed it, but she did.

"Come on then, we'd best go and get you some new football boots I suppose. You had better look after them though David, we aren't made of money you know?"Spot on Mum, you were made of something much more important... love and care. You even gave my boots the odd clean for me every now and then.

"Aww, cheers Mum, you've cleaned my boots, and they look brilliant."

"You'd better score one or two after all that then, hadn't you?" One or two? I'll do my best to rattle a dozen in for you, Mum.

13. WHERE'S WILLY?

Whilst still in the juniors at St. Johns, I remember there was a party at a female school friend's home in a very pleasant area of town. We were collected in a trendy VW camper van by her parents. A rounding up of the privileged few. The young lady was the female equivalent at school of John Walker. She was the focus of many a young chap's attention. There was a pretty even balance of boys and girls at the party. The property was located on Kitty Lane. I kid you not. Kitty Lane. Most, if not all, of the small persons who were classed as female small persons, were delectable little kitten pies. This would bode very well for the kissing games that took place each and every time the room was parentless. When they reappeared, it went straight back to 'Pass the Parcel' and 'Pin the tail on the Donkey'. Not a real Donkey whose tail had dropped off! Lips tightly sealed kissing, of course. None of that slopperty clopperty stuff.

By the end of the party, everyone had pretty much kissed themselves into a hoop. We were herded back into the trendy transport with a lucky bag and a small piece of inedible sponge cake surrounded by white icing sugar several inches thick. It was all very touchy feely, and sitting on knees giggly, in the back of the van as we meandered back for the twelve drop off points. It was cramped and cosy to say the least. My pal Dave ('Willy') Williams decided he would be best served standing up, away from the clutches of his admiring female fans. In a move he no doubt thought was a statement of cool aloofness, he slunk over to the other side of the van on his own. Standing and facing towards us, he then made the error of leaning against the double door exit. To look even cooler, he decided to slide down into more of a half sitting position. The result was the polar opposite of his ambitions. He sat on the handles and the doors swung open. There was a puzzled look of 'What the?' on his face as he disappeared out through the gap like a poorly equipped skydiver. We alerted the driver to the passenger overboard development, and he screeched to a stop.

Willy was still bouncing along the road behind us at thirty miles an hour, rolling over and over like an overpaid Premiership striker. When he finally came to a halt, there were eleven mortified white faces looking sideways out through the doors of the van at our crumpled ex school friend. Dave just stood up and jogged back to the van. A bit embarrassed and red faced he climbed back in. He looked like he'd been hit by a train. Like I said, hard as nails. There was a lot of fuss from the drivers who had swerved to avoid him, and from all of us in the camper van too. He insisted he was okay, despite his arms and legs all pointing in new directions. Anyone aged ten, who throws themselves out of a travelling vehicle and then jogs back and jumps in unfazed, has just secured their place in junior school folklore history. Needless to say, the floor of the camper van was littered with fainted kittens. Damn it! Why hadn't I thought of this stroke of heroic genius and thrown myself out of a moving vehicle. He had a few days off school and came back looking like he'd been cast in the lead role of 'The Mummy'.

He only lived four streets away, so I paid regular visits to check he was still alive and kicking. He was black and blue from head to foot, but found it all hilarious. His Mum was really nice, and spoiling him rotten. He had that same cheeky relationship with his Mum that I had with mine. He could get away with murder almost, with just the threat of boxed ears for being cheeky. I missed my pal at school. We were football, cricket, girl, and music buddies. Dave got me into The Beach Boys, which I think came from the influence of his older brother. We used to listen to 'Barbara Ann' and 'Cotton Fields' all the time. I still love 'Do it again'. Fortunately for Dave, he didn't 'Do it again'. That song still reminds me of hot summers in the Sixties getting into bother with Willy boy.

It was the late Seventies when I started getting into bother in the hot summers with my very own Willy boy. Going to places my Mum and Dad didn't really approve of, pretending I was eighteen with the help of some felt tip pen touch up on my top lip. Parallel trousers with high buttoned waistbands that hopefully distracted females from your spotty greasy face and black ink moustache. Anything to divert them from your appalling dance skills which were akin to someone trying to keep their balance whilst having an epileptic fit on ice. If you were lucky, your hair would be styled into a feather cut, which was all the rage at the time. It was that or a skinhead. I had a near skinhead in a bid to improve the awful feather cut I was given by a trainee hairdresser.

Some of the fashion trends during this era were equally as bad as my haircut. One of my most classic and hilarious outfits of all-time was, twenty-six-inch parallel tartan trousers, a penny round collar shirt with accompanying multi coloured tank top, and a braided blazer with a Lancashire rose badge on the breast pocket. This ensemble was beautifully accessorised with highly polished cherry red Doc Marten boots. I may even have worn yellow elasticated braces to ensure my ridiculous trousers didn't embarrass me by falling down. This ridiculous look, was attempting to carry off a visual statement back then of youthful skinhead menace. It looked more like I had failed as a Lancashire cricketer, and had signed up for Clown College in a bid to secure a job at the circus.

14. BUTLER AND BLAKEY

Back on St. Albans Road, four streets away from where Willy lived, there was my own little gang of mates. My funniest and closest pal by far was John Parker (Blakey). We referred to each other as Butler and Blakey, as we were both of the same opinion that 'On the Buses', the TV comedy sitcom, was hilarious. It was about as funny as trapping your little man in your zip. When John and I first met, we were four or five years old, with only fifty or so yards between our family homes. We have shared the same troubled sense of humour until this very day. We have always held each other in very high disregard, which relentlessly manifested as insults of each other and our families.

Some of our escapades have included things like, posting herring giblets through a random letter box on our way home from setting night lines on the beach. Tying a fellow cub scout to a chair and hoisting him up on some railings outside church. Sprinkling fishing bait maggots on some cakes in a café display cabinet. Assisting a stubborn stand pipe to release its contents of water on a scout camp. Encouraging boxing bouts between reluctant members of our gang for our own amusement. Secreting more herrings (giblets included) into the lining of another friend's coat. Attaching a huge mound of partially chewed chewing gum on the end of a light switch pull in the Gents toilet at youth club. Known in the era of our childhood as boisterous tomfoolery, it is now known today as vandalism, bullying, and criminal insanity.

The secret is, to make sure you've had all of this

rumbustious nonsense completely beaten out of you before you hit the age where custodial sentences will be your reward. Prior to that cut off point, severe reprimands, and the unseen results of your jovial pranks were the only price you would have had to pay. With the odd thick ear thrown in.

Football was the most common interest that brought us all together. We had a core gang of five. Myself, John, Melvin Davis, sadly no longer with us, Steven (Bowie) Beaumont and Richard Davies. It suited John and me perfectly to split any football games massively in our favour. Me and John, stick Melvin, Bowie and Richard. Only one outcome would ever occur, usually along the lines of 26-0. John and I didn't like competing against each other as we had pretty similar abilities. There was way too much of a friendship at stake for bust ups on the pitch to ruin things. Besides we loved crushing our opponents in hopelessly one sided games of mini football. Once, by pure fluke, Melvin, Bowie and Richard inadvertently strung three or four passes together and scored. As Bowie and Richard went galloping around like ponies in spring cheering in wild celebration at the impossible goal they had just crafted, Melvin strolled over to a disbelieving and dumbstruck John and myself. He put an arm around our shoulders, looked us both in the eyes and said, "Dave... John... you made 'em, and thanks." He got a severe arm pummeling for what famously became known as a 'Melvie'. Sentences that sounded as if they came from a seasoned gunslinger in a poor Western.

He loved doing it, you could see the mischief in his face as he felt one coming on. He wouldn't have even finished the sentence before we were chasing him to deliver the standard punishment – a punch to the triceps.

Melvin passed away a few years ago aged 52 from pancreatic cancer. God bless you old friend, our stories remain with us as golden memories.

So there is our gang line up. Me and John as Ronnie and Reggie Kray, Melvin as Tonto. He shouted 'Geronimo' and 'Nagasaki' at the top of his voice for no apparent reason, and followed it up with a punch to your arm. Bowie and Richard made up the five as two terrified underlings who just went along with whatever we suggested, regardless of its legality or threat to their existence. Mostly this entailed hundreds of rounds of unwanted boxing staged by the ruthless promoters (Ronnie and Reggie). We did allow them to wear boxing gloves. We would all get together most afternoons as soon as we had changed our school trousers and shoes. Much to our neighbours' annoyance, it was usually football matches played dangerously close to their windows, gardens and cars. If there were very few, or no, parked cars, we would play lengthways in the street. This gave John and me plenty of room to dribble past Bowie, Richard, and Melvin and increase our goal tally at will. If Melvin stayed in nets, fly goalies were allowed, brushing past Steve and Richard was child's play. If we played short pitch, alleyway to alleyway across the street, they got in the way a lot more, and only triple hat tricks were possible.

Bored with football at times, we'd debate proposals for other activities. It usually came down to water pistol carnage, or bike safari. Sometimes Go-Kart races would be mooted as a third alternative, but this depended heavily on the condition and state of these uncontrollable death traps, as did the supply of pram wheels and timber for the construction stages. The extent of the bike safari was through the back street into Portland Road or Gloucester

Avenue via Ripon Road and back. A distance of two or three hundred metres at most. We had bikes that were too large for us. This was not good for developing testicles, as you had to stretch hard to reach the pedals when in motion. This meant your crotch see sawed very tightly across a rock hard saddle that, depending on the length of journey, slowly gnawed a hole in your scrotum. (This was the thrifty 'they'll grow into them' Sixties.) When you braked to stop, the drop on to the crossbar to touch the floor, inflicted another wallop to your crown jewels. Bowie was still on a smaller bike at that stage, the sort with fat white tyres. Richard had a tiny bike that may well have been pink in colour. Indication of an older sister. Melvin had a Chopper. It was a bicycle version of a Hell's Angel motorbike. Bright orange, with a gear changing facility that neither worked, nor could be understood. It boasted a luxuriously long padded black saddle with a backrest. A proper comfy seat that would surely protect your testicles on journeys over three hundred metres.

Melvin was under strict instructions from his Mum and Dad to never, under any circumstances, let anyone else ever have a go on his bike. John and I got back two days later, having toured the Lake District. Alright, alright, Ripon Road and back. This was with Melvin running alongside of course, shouting to be careful, and definitely not to try and change gears. I changed gears nine times. I think I kept hitting neutral, which would explain how Melvin was able to keep up with me as I tried to speed away and cut loose down Gloucester Avenue. A short scuffle broke out as I alighted back at the departure point. As Melvin and I grappled over the details of my gear changing misdemeanour, John leapt on and peddled off at high speed furiously trying to change gears. The rest of the afternoon was spent fighting. This would usually just involve John, Melvin and myself, with Bowie and Richard smirking knowingly as spectators. It was more like a tag team match between me and John versus Melvin. Melvin had amazing powers of recovery, and even seemed to enjoy being duffed up over and over again by his two pals. When we tired of the wrestling bouts, when Melvin was close to needing medical attention, we would suddenly remember how entertaining it was to watch Bowie and Richard battle to the death over thirty rounds of lightweight championship boxing. Or, until one of them started crying or broke their glasses. As unbiased corner men to them both, John and I pointed out the slim chance of optical related injuries, but it was decided that Richard was better off being able to see where his opponent was at least. If the glasses were knocked from the head, there would be a statutory eight count while they were located, inspected for damage, and returned to the swollen bridge of the nose. If at any time it seemed there could be irreversible eye damage, or either combatant could die due to the catalogue of injuries amassed, then we would make a bell like sound, and allow them a thirty second breather. During this generous interlude, we would pass on advice as to how we thought more blows to the skull may secure victory, for them both. This had the desired effect of making the next round a much more exciting spectacle for the crowd. Which consisted of John, Melvin and me. If Mrs. Davies (Richard's Mum) happened to come out during the bout, she would knock the living daylights out of all of us whilst calmly explaining how I, John and Melvin should have more sense. It seemed a little harsh that she should leather her own son and Bowie too. They had already knocked seven bells out of each other.

15. GING GANG GOOLIES AND GOALIES

Firstly, a little tale from the early Cubs' days. I think there were twelve of us. I was appointed leader of Blue Six, and John was leader of Yellow Six. We wanted to establish among our fellow cubs who could play footy, and what position they played. We were desperate to form a team to play against other local Cub packs. We conducted the interviews like interrogations. When we got to a baby-faced giant of a child with masses of curly blond hair called Anthony, we both thought, 'goalkeeping potential'. This was solely based on his body mass, and not on any knowledge of his cat-like agility between the sticks.

"Hi Anthony, wow you're a big lad pal, do you play any footy, Anthony?"

"Yeah," was the grumpy reply.

"Right, brilliant, that's fantastic, do you fancy playing for the cub team if we manage to get one up and running, Anthony?" we probed further.

"Yeah," was the less than enthusiastic response.

"Fantastic, that's brilliant, Anthony, excellent, great stuff. Where do you play Anthony?"

"In the street." was his unblinking flat toned reply.

John and I exchanged looks of hysterical disbelief at the answer.

"No, we meant what position do you normally play, pal?"

This was met with a blank expression and an awkward silence that spoke volumes about the potential for Anthony to be our very own Gordon Banks. (See ancient Football annuals for reference).

"Fancy being our goalie, Anthony?"

"Yeah," was his single word acceptance speech.

His enthusiasm stretched to an accompanying shrug of his massive shoulders. Think Joe Bugner keeping goal in some Ice Hockey nets. (See ancient boxing books for reference).

To practise and train for upcoming games, John and I used to go down to the park for kickabouts. On full size pitches, and with not another soul around, we would dribble from one end of the pitch to the other while commentating audibly 'Match of the Day' style.

"Hogarth, to Parker, back to Hogarth, to Parker again, back to Hogarth, across to Parker, Parker now, slides it neatly to Hogarth, lovely ball back out to Parker, who again finds Hogarth, back to Parker, super ball through to Hogarth, and oh my god, there it is, what a strike, an unstoppable shot, the keeper could do absolutely nothing about that."

As for a keeper, there wasn't one, just an empty set of full sized posts with no net. We'd go and fetch the ball laughing at how brilliant we were in crafting such a fantastic goal, and then set off back the other way for John to score a cracker down at the other end. This went on for ages until we were knackered or until some adults turned up and required the pitch for a full game with twenty two participants. We were normally faint with hunger by then so would slope off home for tea.

Most of our cub games were played in the freezing cold on Saturday mornings in winter. On one occasion we played on Stanley Park, and it was a partially frozen quagmire from one end of the pitch to the other. How much you were actively involved in the game, dictated just how close to death from freezing you were at the final whistle. John and I would escape with mild hypothermia. Five or six others with severe hypothermia, and three or four requiring immediate hospitalisation.

Funeral services took place for those who had sadly perished in action. This would be after we had showered and returned to the pitch to snap them loose at the ankle. The boots and detached feet were left frozen in the muddy earth. A fitting tribute to their brave footballing sacrifice.

The changing rooms at the Park at best, were brutal, and at worst, somewhere you wouldn't house unloved donkeys. The floor was concrete, awash with the remainder of mud from decades of inept cleaning. It was colder to stand on than having a bag of frozen peas strapped to the sole of each foot. The benches were in fritters, which made sitting down impossible, unless you fancied an arse full of splinters. The coat hooks were vandalised, wobbly, and sharp enough to lacerate any item of clothing you put anywhere near them. You kept your bare feet on your shoes until you got your socks and boots on. Now you were able to stand on ice station zebra to complete changing and being ready to go out. When you came back in however, you were so close to death, that untying boot laces and getting out of your kit was virtually impossible. You couldn't see, hear, or think. You were so cold taking all your gear off to get naked for a shower, that I actually considered showering in my kit and boots, and taking them off later when I was no longer pale blue and hallucinating.

My Dad (Les) and John's Dad (Barrie) would always come down to watch us play. They got roped in either refereeing or running the line, helping with the kit bag and drinks for half time. Putting nets up. If you have never whacked a ball into a netted goal, you haven't lived. An additional duty for my Dad included having to assist Richard, the bespectacled lightweight boxer of slight build and polite manner, to undress and get into the shower. As if this wasn't bad enough, when he re-emerged from the shower looking like death warmed up, he asked of my Dad,

"Please, Mr. Hogarth, could you dry me as well?"

God bless him. (My Dad used to call Richard, Godfrey, after the Dad's Army character. He was a child version of the role to a tee. Mannerly, polite, and unassuming. Not your usual lightweight boxing type).

When you did dare to tip toe at breakneck speed into the shower, you were not welcomed by Premiership quality wet room facilities. There were eight shower heads. Only three of which worked at half normal water pressure. The other five ranged between a steady dripping action and the agonising trickle of a penis with kidney stones. There was a writhing huddle of muddy survivors' at the most powerful streams of lukewarm water. Here, you would jostle for position, hoping a splash or two of life saving warmth would land on your shivering torso and dribble down your legs to allow some degree of cleansing and comfort. Others would stand isolated under dripping broken plumbing, staring ahead in the hope that death would rescue them from this self- inflicted water torture.

We did usually win most of our games, but there were some other Cub packs who had much feared and skilled tough nuts in their ranks. For the purposes of protection for those games, we very wisely drafted in my pal Dave Williams for guest appearances. I have no idea how Dave gained his reputation as someone not to mess with. By beating the holy living daylights out of bullies who picked on him, I suppose. But he had a wonderful calming influence around other hard cases. A local bully two or three years older than Dave once tracked him down to give him a tanking. Dave never wanted any trouble, he was a proper good lad, moral and fair, he hated bullies. He warned this kid to leave him alone or he would hurt him. Dave ended up taking this lad's belt off and lashing him with it until he begged for mercy. It meant nothing to Dave at all. He wasn't bothered, and he wasn't interested. A few big kids got a nasty shock when they pushed our Willy boy over the edge.

There was talk regarding one fixture we had arranged that we were going to get a duffing, before, during, and after the game. Thankfully Davey boy was available. He loved to face up to that sort of challenge. He would never instigate anything though. Hard and fair. Shake hands after the game. Well played lads, win or lose. Gracious in defeat and a great player too. The two who were going to do the duffing up, were as nice as pie all game. I think they beat us 5-3. It was one changing room for both teams, and there wasn't a word out of turn. The two lads chirped up on their way past us.

"Cheers lads, thanks for the game." They didn't eyeball Dave at all. Dave stuck his hand out. "Cheers lads, thanks a lot." They shook his hand and managed a respectful smile and nod of the head. That's just how it should be, both in life, and in sport.

It's so sad that doesn't seem to be around much anymore. Dog eat dog, win at all costs, trample on all and sundry to reach the top. Makes me angry and admit that losing my way for a while has had a lot to do with the world at large. Mum would always point me back in the direction of hope and optimism though. She had an amazing way of ignoring all the bad stuff and focusing on the positive.

"I have faith, David, you doubt everything you see and

hear, and always have done. Faith isn't something to see or hear. Faith is what you believe in, it's in your heart, and always will be. You choose, son."

"Do you mean like the way I chose a new pair of footy boots?"

"You don't listen sometimes, do you? You can't be serious for five minutes David."

You'd be surprised, Mum, I listened to every word you ever said, and still do.

shirt and tie party, 1965

16. CAMP APOCALYPSE

Now, where were we? Oh yes, in the Cubs. An organisation my Mum was very keen to get me enrolled into for all sorts of sensible reasons. Mainly to get me out from under her feet. It would teach me valuable lessons for later in life, such as, being able to start a fire (for when I'm cold and homeless). To be competent at knot tying (which will prevent my hostages from escaping), and having a clean handkerchief in my pocket for when I inexplicably burst into tears on an alarmingly regular basis. Fire, rope, and crying? What could possibly go wrong?

Her intentions were good, and in Cubs I would learn teamwork, discipline, helpfulness, compassion, and earn small amounts of money by pretending to sweep old ladies back yards on bob a job week. Sometimes you didn't get money, just a handful of buttons and bird seed.

One of a good Cub's tools of the trade, was of course, a trusty sheath knife. Mine had the nasty habit of slicing me open if I even dared to look at it. John had one as well, and he was even more prone to cutting himself to ribbons. Most of the time we went camping was spent recovering from knife wounds. Sitting under trees in the shade with lemonade and a hanky tied around a bloody digit. Lemonade and a hanky are essential to recover from a sliced thumb. These were decent sized knives. We had an inbuilt desire to stab, slice, and whittle anything that stood in our way. Except other fellow cub scouts of course. This was the sixties, not modern day Britain.

In the minibus, on the journey up to the lakes, we looked like anxious commandos, heading to a life or death situation somewhere in Cumbria. Just what the trees and nature of the area had done to deserve our visit is beyond comprehension, but there was some serious chopping, slicing, and stabbing to be done. When the minibus finally came to a halt at Great Tower Scout Camp, the doors burst open at the back, spewing out ten year olds the likes of which this protected beautiful National Park had never seen before. It was like 'Raid on Entebbe', only it was 'Bowness on Windermere'. We didn't just have deadly sheath knives. We were also allowed access to hand axes, and felling axes. Have you ever seen so many choppers all at once? We were hell bent on damage and destruction on an industrial scale.

Our early visits to this camp site saw us housed in pine smelling dorm huts. Sleep in these luxurious cabins came when you either passed out from excited exhaustion, or another cub you may be battling with, swung a lucky blow. We did graduate to hike tents outdoors when a little older and our bodies had become more resistant to hypothermia. Those tents were of a size that two poorly fed door mice would struggle to squeeze into. We were billeted three to a tent, so it was snug to say the least.

John and I always had plans to be up early to be able to sneak off and hunt deer. When I say hunt, I simply mean, attempt to pursue them noisily on foot. In full camouflage, and faces blackened, we headed off like native Indian scouts in pursuit of our quarry, but were soon wandering through the woods aimlessly, getting hopelessly lost and having to shout for help. We were armed with spears, bows and arrows, axes and sheath knives. If we had come across any hostile hillbillies, they would have cacked themselves and run for the hills. Some other hills, a bit farther away. We looked like extras who had got lost during the filming of 'Apocalypse Now' and had ended up in the Lake District. This was Cumbria for Christ's sake, not Vietnam.

The weapons we had crafted for ourselves from sustainable local materials (vandalised some trees without permission), were terrifying. The spears were trimmed, balanced, and whittled to a point, then tempered secretly in the hot ashes of the camp fire. The arrows received similar fine tuning, and had bracken leaves attached with twine for flights. They were so potent these weapons of ours that we had to store them in a secure undisclosed location off site. Our expert knowledge of tracking and hunting deer, was second to none, and armed with all our expertise, (get down wind of them), we headed for Eagle rock with the prospect of venison for supper. We tracked a herd for ten minutes – a stag and maybe as many as ten females. They were fully grown and so agile across the steep hillsides, it was glorious to watch. The stag was a big fella, and had magnificent antlers. He would stop every so often and glance around sniffing the air for the scent of danger. He must have had a heavy cold that week for him not to smell two sweaty cubs stumbling around noisily a hundred metres downwind. I must also assume he had cataracts, as he didn't see us either. This seems impossible, as we were unable to keep still for five seconds.

When the mission failed, and we became wet, cold, and hungry, we relied on our cub intuition and used the smell of cooking bacon to guide us back to camp. The bacon butties were fantastic.

Later on that day, in the early evening, we returned to another spot where we had noticed a huge number of innocent rabbits seemed to congregate. They were there to catch up on local gossip and to exercise their loins in the interests of the survival of their species. With all the stealth and skill of useless cubs with deluded intentions, we approached with our spears at the ready to bag some supper. As darkness fell, spotters with Pifco torches readied themselves to flood the glen with shimmering beams of death. More light would have been radiated, by a poorly Glow-worm who had forgotten that he still had his coat on.

"Ready?... Ready?... Now!"

We shouted, as a signal for the searchlights to be engaged. The misty sheen of pale yellow light, was just about enough for you to be able to make out the writhing orgy of potential casserole ingredients at play. It was like a scene from a rabbit version of Caligula. Then we would charge, shouting and screaming like the blood thirsty savages that we were. The rabbits dissolved into the night seamlessly at blurring speed. We collected our inaccurately hurled spears, turned off the torches, and lay in wait silently, until the furry vulgarity recommenced. The process was repeated until the batteries in the torches died completely. Twice more, at most.

Supper was tinned beans with sausages. Then dough twists on a twig, held in the campfire until perfectly cooked. They were usually raw inside, and burnt to a crisp on the outside. When you bit into them under the watchful gaze of responsible Scout leaders, your mouth would be subjected to an assault of molten pastry hotter than the sun. It would attach itself to your gums and teeth through the process of nuclear fusion, and incinerate all flesh and taste buds that it came into contact with. Your face now gave the impression that you were smiling in delight at this delicious camp fire delicacy. This was not so. Very much akin to the Joker in the Batman movies, you were now left with a permanent open mouthed half grin come grimace and wild staring eyes. Closing your mouth for the next couple of weeks would be impossible. All of this would now be accompanied by a hopping and screaming pow-wow like dance around the camp fire, that would convince others to join in. They assumed you were merely trying to get things going for the evening. This was not so, either. It was simply an outpouring of scalded agony interpreted through the mediums of song and dance.

There was one last mission for the evening, to get your sheath branded. The event took place at the camp HQ. Not inside the hut I might add, but at a small serving hatch that opened up twice daily to satisfy the mile long queue of easily pleased cubs with nothing better to do. Sheath branding, was really the only reason you had come to camp. The hatch was down the long side of the cabin. To avoid hysteria, and crowd trouble, there was a sign with the strict rules of engagement written on it in red. The do's and do nots of expected behaviour regarding this process were both complex and unnecessary. Wait in line, hand the man your sheath with the correct money, and allow him to brand it with his red hot iron. Forty minutes standing in line talking about how great this was, and how you couldn't wait to get your sheath branded. When I did finally get to the branding hatch, the blind idiot stuck it in the wrong place and it was smudged. Well, that was a waste of thirty pence. Not only that. I now had a sheath that wasn't worth a toss. The hatch did serve another purpose, it opened at totally different times in the whole new guise of a tuck shop. The hatch was too high up for anyone to see in properly, so a game of, *"Have you got?"*, *"No"* went on for hours with the kid in front who only had twenty-three pence! Not even enough to get his sheath branded. Just get some wriggly worms kid and do one will you. Our turn.

"Are you doing branding now?"

"No, just the times on the sign."

"There's a sign of the times?"

"Yep."

"What is it?"

"What's what?"

"The sign of the times?"

"It's a sign with the times on."

"Where?"

"There." He points to the sign with a hint of impatience.

"Oh right yeah, err, got any pork lollies, or ham cycles?"

"What's a ham cycle?"

"About ten miles a day, if it's sunny."

"Ha ha, very funny, come on lads, what do you want?"

"Two cokes, two salt and vinegar crisps, and two mars bars please, Marlon"

"Marlon? Why Marlon? My name's... oh right, I get it, right little pair of comedians you two aren't you? Here, go on, piss off, go and do some whittling or something."

We leave with our supplies that will be stored and consumed later, after night manoeuvres, and a midnight trek to Eagle rock, where a few of the renegades would convene to tell packs of scout camp lies, pretend to enjoy smoking, and hopefully impress a rebellious girl guide or two.

The visits to Eagle rock drew a blank for John and me in terms of pulling a Girl Guide. We were too young, and just at that age where you pretended you knew what it was all about, but didn't. You would always hope no one would suddenly corner you and interrogate you about how much you knew. Nothing, was the answer. We would sit around chatting with other young bucks and you would hear all sorts of highly unlikely rubbish.

There were some older scouts at camp with us. They were camp leaders who you would not dare disobey. Unless you were John and myself, in which case you just ignored them and did as you pleased. They had access to the felling axes. They were two real characters, Mick and Stan. They were seven or eight years older than us, smoked, had mopeds, and kissed girls. We saw them at Youth Club, and Eagle Rock. You had to be damn sneaky to catch them. They would wander off with a smitten young lady on the moody premise of showing them something interesting in the woods. There was a chance from a position of stealth, sixty feet up a tree, to observe the magical coming together of innocent lips. To pick up tips from sixty feet away, surrounded by thick foliage and bewildered Owls and Squirrels is no mean feat. It appeared, from our hugely dicey vantage point, that their heads had become stuck together. Even from as far away as we were, the sound of slurping sloppiness in the moonlit dark was making one owl very nervous. The others didn't give a hoot (okay, I'll get my coat). It went on for ages. Eventually, and with a sound that resembled a very wet stubborn Octopus being dragged off a plate glass window, the world record attempt at face eating, came to an oxygen deprived end. John and I had seen enough of this boring nonsense, and decided we should be away chopping things with an axe. We bid the owls and squirrels goodnight, and shinned down the branches like seasoned tree toppers who had heard the dinner bell. We were back in our tent before dawn, and the rising of the camp elders. They would come around to do a body count first thing in the morning, making sure we were all present and correct.

"Come on sleepy heads, rise and shine, up you get, it's

ten to eight. Time to get this campfire going, and get some breakfast on."

We had only been back about an hour and had just dozed off. First job was wandering around looking for kindling to get the fire up and running. We would shuffle around picking up dry twigs of various sizes that would be perfect to turn smouldering ashes into a furnace. This usually required, in addition, a good slug of petrol, which was far less labour intensive, and produced instant results.

Had we relied on the traditional two stick and string pulley technique, we would have been found years later by explorers and named - *Group of frozen dead men and boys looking at sticks*. The accompanying Attenborough like voice over may well have sounded, thus: "This primitive group of near Neanderthals were clueless when it came to survival. The sheer number of rabbits in this area, is indeed testament to their poor aim and lack of ability for stealth when it came to hunting. Their tools were crude and unrefined, and as you can see by their stupid and gormless expressions, death and extinction were inevitable. Here, this group of older and younger males have been attempting to start a fire. Their ineptitude with regard to the skill required, and the lack of intelligence to realise just how cold it was getting, are sadly the reason this brief dim race, known as Homo Stupendous very quickly ran out of time. If only they'd had some petrol and a lighter, things may have turned out differently. But It was not to be, as Mick, had gone to the off-licence on his moped to get some more fags and cider."

"What are you lot trying to do?" said Mick, with a lit fag in his mouth and a five litre tin of petrol. We stood back while he splashed fuel on dead ashes and lots of damp sticks. He took a last drag of his fag, and flicked it onto the sad mound of lifeless timber. Whoosh, we were all engulfed in a pleasantly warm fireball of campfire arson.

"One of you clowns put a pan of water on, I'm dying for a brew," Mick said,

walking off to put the fuel away.

There was excited talk over breakfast that we'd been promised a go at tree felling. Supervised and legal, of course, which took the edge off it for John and me, but a chance to wield the mighty felling axe was not to be missed. The man responsible for the supervision of this event was the Head Warden at Great Towers. There were no other Wardens. It was a role he occupied alone. He was not a man of jovial nature. He told you off at times, just for being there. He looked like a cross between Bill Oddie and James Galway. He didn't like birds, nor did he play the flute. In the entire time of the expedition to find suitable trees for us to hack at, his voice remained at a constant low psychopathic tone. It was like listening to a tape recording of a serial killer's confession who had been given extra medication to avoid becoming over agitated. Tree chopping wasn't going to be a happy, fun event, with enjoyable memories. It was going to be a serious clinical destruction of timber with meticulous precision. If not, Mrs. Head Warden would be in for a less than memorable evening after supper, but presumably, there was no Mrs. Head Warden either. Just a squeaky rocking chair in the attic window of the cabin, with the shrouded corpse of an old lady who watched silently over the forest and all its goings on.

We finally arrived at a spot that Bill Galway deemed a suitably safe environment for supervised tree felling by the correct application of precise axe incursions. Listen pal, just make with the felling axes and get out of the way, you donut, we all thought, as we smiled and nodded in awe at the depth and breadth of his mind-numbing lack of personality. The pre-hack lecture went on and on and on, until I pretended to faint from boredom to get things moving. It became clear, that the extent of his health and safety monologue were in fact valid, and possibly too short, as scout after scout flayed away dangerously with the axes like Vikings on steroids.

Some actually missed the trees altogether, and swung themselves completely off their feet. Happily they maintained a hold of the axe, or there could have been some stories to explain to Mums and Dads who were hoping to collect whole children when we returned home from camp.

"Hello there, yes he's fine Mrs. Davies, just a bit of a nick that's all. Kid's eh? His head is here in this plastic carrier bag. He'll be fine with a bit of Mum's home cooking and a good night's sleep."

Bill Galway decided that precise tree incursions should be limited to the bigger stronger cubs and scouts. There weren't any. We did manage to chop a couple of smaller innocent trees to pieces. All in the name of correct tree husbandry of course. The venom with which Bill Galway struck the trees while in demo mode, painted more of a picture of dismembered victims behind a secret panel at his log store, and a wife who had absconded many years since.

Practice with choppers over, we headed back to camp with Bill grinding his teeth in between his running commentary on the forest and its many hidden lurking dangers. *Yeah, you! You psycho*. With a grim smile that would have frightened Zulus, Bill bid us good day and left us at a crossroads of trail paths to head back to his cabin in the woods. No doubt to make some soup for the watcher in the attic, and to carve nymphs and animals of the forest from his store of human bones. Or, he may well have had a quick shower, and gone down into Bowness for a nice pint and a bite to eat before going to see 'Butch Cassidy and the Sundance Kid' at the local cinema. Either way, he was as mad as a biscuit. He was covered in scout award badges to prove it. I'll swear one said, 'Clinically Insane with Merit'. He also helped out with branding duties if Marlon was swamped.

John and I were expelled from scouts aged eleven, for tying about fifty bangers together, and throwing the entire package into a soon to start scout meeting. Cubs and scouts emerged from the church hall staggering and coughing. Their blackened soot strewn faces and smouldering clothing was evidence that we may have underestimated the power of our amusing prank. We received a severe warning and a ceremonial removal of our toggles, neckerchiefs and badges, before appearing before a court martial committee for dismissal. Ironically, we were awarded our 'Clinically Insane with Merit' badges at the same ceremony. Only to have them cruelly snatched back immediately after, for being clinically insane. We were now very close to the age when being in the scouts was a sure fire way of getting yourself duffed up at school for being a do-gooding cub-scout pansy.

17. RAINDROPS KEEP FALLING ON MY HEAD

As it happens, one of my favorite movies of all time is 'Butch Cassidy and the Sundance Kid', which I was determined to see as a ten year old despite its 'A' rating, and reluctance from my Mum to take me. Under eleven meant you had to be accompanied by an adult. Mum preferred historical dramas and had already dragged me to see 'Henry the Eighth' (nice lad!) 'Cromwell' (ditto) 'The Flame and the Arrow' (sword fights galore) 'The Prince of Donegal' (sword fights galore in Ireland) 'The Man in the Iron Mask' (sword fights galore in masks)... you get the picture.

Eventually, after days of trying to convince her that she would enjoy it, and that they were actually a pair of misunderstood lovable rogues who robbed the rich to give to the poor, a bit like Robin Hood, I finally got the nod for a matinee run.

"Honest Mum, they only kill people if they really have to, and they mostly do banks not people's houses. Not bad lads really, a bit like me and John." I just got 'the look' for that comparison.

"Well I hope it's not just all noisy shooting and fighting all the time David, you watch enough of that sort of rubbish as it is." The body count in my Mum's films very easily outstripped Butch and Sundance by quite some margin.

I remember the afternoon we went to see it very well, we caught the bus into town and walked along to the Odeon on Dickson Road. I tried to keep a discreet distance from Mum in case other lads my age saw me and thought

I was out shopping with her. I got closer to her in the foyer when a hot dog, a Pepsi and a box of fruit gums were required. It was a big cinema the Odeon, and it was pretty busy too, so we sat over on the left side where the seats were quieter. There is nothing worse than a noisy seat when you're trying to watch a movie, is there? They were the fold down type, whose comfort padding had given up and left years ago. It was like sitting on a box full of old engine parts covered with a tea towel. They had once been plush and luxuriant, covered with dark red velvet and cushioning a foot thick.

I was always fascinated by the safety curtain at the Odeon. It was a pinky orange golden colour with sparkly golden orbs dotted about towards the bottom. I used to squint my eyes at it like I did with our Christmas tree lights.

When the film started, I was horrified to observe that it appeared to be in black and white, or sepia if you want to be totally accurate. I complained to Mum immediately and threatened that I would leave if things didn't damn well buck up sharpish. I was told not to be silly, and that it was bound to be in colour in a few minutes. It was. Damn clever these Mums you know. I then settled back into my agonising death trap of a sedan and stared open mouthed and unblinking for the entire film. Mum did pop the odd fruit gum into my mouth for me so I didn't dry up completely.

At the end of the film, and even with my limited intelligence, I had the vague feeling that things hadn't ended well for our intrepid heroes. This could not be. In a state of disbelieving stressed mental meltdown, I quizzed Mum for the entire journey home as to how they must have made good their escape and returned triumphant to slaughter the entirety of the Bolivian army. There was no such good news. Not even from my Mum. Sometimes, things just don't end up happily ever after every time. You may never actually find what it is you are looking for... ever. That is why it is vitally important that you at least enjoy the search.

As they sit in the bullet riddled building shot to pieces, patching each other up at the end of the movie, they still believe, and they still have plans. Australia, is Butch's last great suggestion.

"It's a long way isn't it?" Sundance responds. "Arghh, it's always got to be perfect with you."

"I just don't want to get there and find it stinks... that's all".

"Well if we never try, or go and look, we'll never know anything, will we?"

Before they face the final hopeless shoot-out, Butch suddenly gives them one last glimmer of hope.

"Hey, you didn't see Lafors out there did you?" Butch asks. "No," replies Sundance. "Good... for a minute there I thought we were in trouble."

Ready?

Ready.

18. LIGHT THE BLUE TOUCH PAPER

When it came to the winter months as a kid, I was a real big fan of Bonfire night. Fizz, bang, whoosh, crack, ping, bang poop, (And those were just the noises coming from my trousers). The dangers and the excitement were always at fever pitch approaching November 5th. We would always obediently follow the firework code, and do our best not to kill anyone we knew. We had a very trusty and safety conscious biscuit tin for storage of our non-fatal pyrotechnics. The tin was more dangerous than the fireworks. It had very sharp edges. It was about two foot by a foot, and had a blue mosaic background with coloured crowns and golden chalice's all over it. A special Christmas Peek Frean's homage to the little baby Jesus, limited edition. The perfect container for a selection of tasty treats originally, and now for dangerous explosives.

Some of the names were odd; Snowdrops, Golden Shower, Whistle-stop, Instant Incineration. Mum would store all of the bigger box type fireworks in the cupboard where she kept the highly flammable cleaning products, paraffin and spare matches, all nice and safe. Don't be silly, David, that didn't happen. Alright, alright, it was just paint thinners (that I used to love sniffing). These were the big finale fireworks that cost a packet and had names more befitting of an arson attack on Parliament. Crackpot Crackerjack Cascade, Wham Bam Ka-boom, Ballistic Blitzkrieg. I'm sure Mum frowned and shook her head when I pointed them out behind the glass display whilst slavering with unhinged madness in my eyes. I had quite a lot of sugar on my porridge that morning. My sister brought us back down to earth by requesting a Katherine Wheel. In a flash I requested a David Wheel, and have been ridiculed every November 5th since, for being daft.

John and I would construct a Guy for the purpose of embezzling money out of gullible local shoppers. Our Guy actually looked like he had already been hung drawn and quartered. He certainly didn't look like a man in robust health, who was capable of mass murder on an explosively industrial scale. For his face we cleverly utilised a skull Halloween mask. It was attached via an elastic cord around a balloon. For added character he was accessorised with a tweed trilby hat at a jaunty angle to indicate casual impudence and hatred for the establishment. He resembled an emaciated door to door salesman in need of a good supper.

After upsetting most of the elderly lady shoppers in the area, we decided on some cheerful adjustments to improve our takings. Off came the skull face and a bigger orange balloon was used for his head. We drew a bearded smiling Guy Fawkes in felt tip pen. The result was a happy, sunburnt terrorist. It worked though, and very soon we had enough money to buy cider, chips, and chocolate. We transported the suntanned lunatic around in an old tartan shopping trolley that had belonged to my Gran. Our pitch outside the off-licence was a great spot to collar embarrassed alcoholics into parting with loose change. Anything to get away from the scene quickly with their clanking carrier bags full of shame. They weren't clad a great deal better than our Guy, who we'd fashioned in some old track suit bottoms and a natty Fair Isle sweater that Mum thought was lovely, but I'd refused to wear. My plan was to see it in flames come bonfire night. His ensemble was completed with a pair of brown suede Hush

Puppies shoes that my Dad was unaware he no longer had a need for. The trilby hat was his as well. It was not your usual look for around 1605, but his tragic appearance had us coining it in. Most of the funds we raised went on bangers. These simply went bang, once. They did have a few seconds of fizz prior to the bang. This tempted you to be stupid enough to hold on to it for a few seconds before hurling it into some poor old blighter's back yard. There would be the obligatory bang followed by the anguished meow of a traumatised cat. To a ten year old these bangers were mini sticks of dynamite, and there was tons of stuff that needed blowing up. Guy Fawkes' head and imaginary Nazis for starters.

Come the big day itself you couldn't wait to get home from school and re-examine your tinned arsenal. I would take each firework out in turn and read of their ingredients and damage potential in great detail like a highly trained bomb disposal expert, only the complete opposite. I was keen to witness mass explosions of a colourful kind. We had quite an array of rockets, should our street require defending against an invasion at any point during the evening. These required a small launch pad arrangement that was achieved by pushing a milk bottle into the soil. The stick of the rocket slipped neatly into the little hole, which in reality was a lot less filthy than it sounds. Light the blue touch paper, and whoosh! A one way ticket to the stars. Or, the roof of the garden shed at my Gran's house two streets away.

With all this whizzing, whooshing and banging going on, it was wise to keep your pets well out of harm's way. But Judy loved fireworks and I would lift her on to the back living room table so she could watch out of the window. Perhaps I had stroked the part of her brain flat that would normally cause her to run a mile at such a commotion. Spending time around me had numbed her fear of chaos. The fireworks were like a blissful calming relief for her.

The ceremony of lighting each and every firework was exclusively down to my Dad. Maybe my Mum would be allowed to light a snowdrop or sparkler when assisted and supervised, but this was man's work. Mum was in charge of baked potatoes, parkin, treacle toffee and hot dogs. I would load up with so much treacle toffee that my mouth required wrenching open every bonfire night about every ten minutes.

"Stop putting so much toffee in your mouth David, you're just being silly." Correct, Mum.

There was the usual duff firework drama of the one that had been alight and then gone out. This meant that Dad would have to render the stubborn waste of money completely safe by stamping on it for about an hour. We would watch open mouthed as he would appear to re-enact a traumatic flash back to the second world war battlefield ensuring that the enemy was no longer a threat to mankind. He needed tea and a huge slice of parkin after his Mexican hat dance to restore blood sugar levels.

Any fireworks which came with special lifesaving instructions such as '*Place on a high flat surface and emigrate*' were treated with extra care and respect. Once ignited they would launch with vindictive menace straight towards any gathering of sparkler waving innocents. My sister's Katherine wheel was nailed to the fence per instructions, and was a huge success until we realised it had set fire to the fence. Dad had to throw water on it. I have a suspicion he was disappointed that he couldn't stamp on it. He calmed down after a hot dog and some treacle toffee. The finale was reserved for the biggest rocket and the last big expensive firework. The rocket usually veered off at a crazy angle and was enjoyed by people in the next county, exploding with bangs and flashes that left you blind and deaf for weeks.

Better to go out with a bang than get trampled underfoot or be drenched with cold water. Don't be silly, David, Mum would say. Her wonderful shining bright light faded and dimmed as she gently slipped away. Quite amazing though that in my darkest moments, she still shines for me like the brightest star in the sky.

19. WHEN YOU WISH

When we weren't making hopeless guys or posting fish giblets through letter boxes, John and I had to content ourselves with other pastimes. We would listen to the best that the pop pickers charts had to offer, think about girls, and how best to irritate or impress them, and take full advantage of any heavy snowfalls in the winter months by pounding anything that moved, with snowballs. A new family with a four-daughter surplus moved into our street one winter, and there was further rumour that they were Welsh. Our ears did eventually tune in to their dialect. In the meantime we used a lot of wild gesturing and increased voice volume as if we were trying to communicate with early humans who had just emerged from the undergrowth wearing nothing but open mouthed bewilderment.

"Oop 'ere int' Narth Wist," we would shout at them, and then describe some local customs.

"And that's 'ow it is oop 'ere flower," we would reassure them, leaving them blinking with blank expressions. After a few seconds of bewildered silence they would all burst into fits of laughter and point at us. Then we asked what their names were, and it was our turn to laugh and point. John actually dislocated his lower jaw having a go at one of the names. We eventually settled on 'The Taffies' as a group description, and a simple numbering system for individuals. The oldest taffy was the one John and I had ear marked as potential romantic material. Not that we had a clue about how, what or why. Her name had the handy short version Del, which we replaced into a song's lyrics so we could sing. 'Tonight,

tonight, and every night, I'm going to snog Del Taffy'. Needless to say this did not happen on any night, ever.

We had little gangs that would form in those days, then break up two days later over arguments about nothing. Our band of five stuck together though, no matter what. There were plenty of fall outs and punch ups, but we would be back together as a unit pretty quickly.

A lot of our winter evenings playing out, would involve stealth like war games. They were a slightly more violent version of hide and seek. The quarry would be sent off and given the task of getting back to a base area, whilst avoiding being jumped on and clubbed half to death. There was no reason for us to jump on them and club them, we just rather liked it. They would be sent a few streets away and then told to get back unscathed and as sneakily as possible. John and I would climb into some outrageous spots to avoid detection. When the passing whispering victims were directly below, we would leap off garage roofs and ageing apple tree branches to administer a good clubbing before dragging the hapless prisoners back to base for interrogation.

This brutal behaviour may well have been influenced by a TV show at the time called 'Garrison's Guerrilla's', whose main purpose as a band of misfit mercenaries, appeared to be to kill everyone else in every episode. They succeeded every show, without a scratch on any of them. Saturday teatime TV slaughter at its finest. When I was finally shouted in by Mum from the horrors of war on the street, I would be sent up for a bath before 'The Val Doonican Show' came on at eight.

These were the days of three channels on telly and no remote control. As the youngest member of our clan, I was up and down like a yo-yo, pushing buttons and turning knobs. As a special treat on Saturday evenings the telly was allowed to make the short journey into our lounge, a room that was only to be used for special occasions, or when we had visitors such as Christmas day, or when Uncle Ronnie and Auntie Jenny came around two or three times a year. Kate and I had applied pressure for the luxury of the lounge to be used more regularly as it was a much nicer room, with wallpaper, seats, and carpet. All this was a bit of a chore according to my Dad, as it meant unplugging the telly and carrying it some thirty feet into the lounge. The aerial had to be unplugged, and the magazines needed to be taken off the shelf under the TV table. Hang on Dad, you drove a tank in World War Two, I think we can manage to get the telly thirty feet into the lounge! He resisted us getting a colour TV for many years. His argument was, watching cricket and snooker in colour just wouldn't be the same! No that's right Dad, it would be in colour. I later discovered he was colour blind and couldn't see red and green very well. God bless you, Dad.

The ceremony was formal. All doors propped open prior to departure. Signals to be given if a rest was required due to fatigue. Lift on the count of three etc. The women folk had been removed from the area for their own safety. As we started to lift I got the shock of my life. It was like lifting a cast iron safe full of gold bullion. Dad went backwards, I went crimson. At the end of the thirty feet my face was purple and my fingers numb. So this was why we watched our only telly in the back room all the time.

The other special Saturday night treat was the awesome beauty of the two bar coal effect electric fire. Rarely used, and only for celebrations, when we had company, or were very close to freezing to death. It was so powerful and mighty that one bar was plenty, according to Dad. If Mum or I would dare to put the second bar on, it was only to be for a few minutes as we would all roast, according to Dad. His famous saying was, 'If you're cold, put some clothes on'. He must have meant, hat, coat, gloves, scarf etc. as I recall I was actually fully clothed already. Electricity was only to be used in emergencies. That's right, a bit like modern day Britain is today.

"Give the coals a blow David, the discs have stopped turning." my Mum would instruct. They've seized up from lack of use, I would think.

"That's better, it looks much nicer when they're going round."

You're right Mum, it sure did. The final big treat for the night was turning the big light off. It made Dad happy, for one. All four of us cosy and snug, the couch pulled up, Dad on his chair, the coal effect fire sweeping orange patterns across our faces as we watched Val Doonican and his twinkling Irish eyes singing 'Paddy McGinty's Goat'. We had all we could wish for. Lucky boy, very lucky boy indeed (Not Val Doonican, me).

20. AN ENGLISHMAN ABROAD

I didn't just confine my stupidity to this country. Well, mostly I did, but it was now the era of the foreign package holiday, and a chance to be, quite literally, an idiot abroad. As a family we usually took holidays in Canterbury where my Dad's sister lived. Or Bournemouth or Torquay or Anglesey. Traditional British holidays that were always a great deal of fun. It was now all the trend to go abroad though, and to ensure we kept up with the Jones's, whoever they were, we began mentioning at meal times just how fantastic it would be to go on our first holiday to the sun.

First things first though. We had to persuade my Dad that it wasn't all foreign muck they ate, and we would still be able to drink tea and enjoy HP sauce too. They did have HP sauce, thank goodness, and we were forced to smother the muck and flavour our tea with it.

I could be wrong, but I seem to remember Dad sending his Gazpacho soup back because it was "stone cold". Our other challenge to even get a holiday to Spain booked, was to avert Dad's gaze from the grid at the bottom of the page that had the prices in it. End of July, one week, for two adults and two children. Thirty-seven pounds fifty, including flights, accommodation, all cold food, excursions and ants.

"Don't be silly, David, it cost more than that."

"Oh, hi Mum, yes you're right it did, about eighty quid I think?"

Dad had to go and have a lie down on the settee in the lounge with the curtains drawn for an hour to recover.

"David?"

"Alright, alright, he got his cheque book out and sent the correct amount off to the travel agents with just the tiniest amount of fear and trepidation flickering in his eyes."

With only nine months to wait until we went, I could barely contain my excitement. So much so that I looked at the picture of our hotel about a hundred times a day. I had already picked out the spot where I was going to lounge by the pool, and parade my sporty ten-year old physique in my Rawcliffe's summer range swimming trunks. As with all trips to trendier foreign lands, they were the polar opposite of what the bronzed local kids wore with casual superiority. Damn my pale blue band, white band, navy blue band, box type shorts with little golden anchor on the leg of the left thigh. It was a wonder I didn't get my head kicked in. My sickly translucent white flesh and stork like legs must have gained me enough pity to be ignored as a complete non-threat to any of the local Senoritas. The ones who were ten years old, at least.

The whole process of wading through the arm full of holiday brochures that Mum had brought back from town, was epic. It was only ever going to be Majorca, but where?

After weeks of family debates around the open booklets on the dining room table between the hours of six thirty and nine in the evening, the final decision was circled heavily in biro. There was the addition of a large arrow pointing down to the price table where the cost was also circled alongside a big star drawn in my Dad's hand. Hotel Portals in Portals Nous was our final preferred choice. God help them. God help them all.

I was so excited, that I decided to start checking my extensive (very small) summer wardrobe, for a yes, no, maybe, piles system. I had one maybe, and seven no's. I concluded that I may have been too harsh, and after a quick rejig, ended up with eight 'no's. How has that happened?! I think me and you are heading into town at some point Mumsie, to purchase some high-end fashion items that will show those Spanish youngsters just what cool looks like.

It was only on arrival in Spain that I would be proved horribly wrong, and the painful truth would become irrefutably apparent. Instead of cutting the look of casual impudent renegade, I rather more resembled a very smart young English chap whose flesh had never once seen the light of day.

As summer approached, I upped my body building schedule to two press ups and four sit ups a day. The placebo effect this had in my mind was amazing. I went around lifting things up for absolutely no reason, only to hastily put them back down before permanent muscle damage occurred. With my ears ringing, and those little white rods pinging around in my vision, I would quiz mother, "What do you think about that then, eh?" This was my attempt to not only convince Mum that I was old enough to travel to foreign lands, I was strong enough too.

"You'll put your back out if you're not careful, and put that vacuum cleaner down David, you're turning purple."

"I'll take it upstairs for you Mum, if you like?" I wheezed through gritted teeth, as I started off down the hallway with my legs slowly turning to jelly. Before I reached the foot of the stairs, I collapsed and passed out in a heap with the vacuum cleaner clearly the victor of this particular test of strength. As Mum slapped my gormless face back to life, I mumbled incoherently about how I must have got my foot tangled in the cord and cracked my head on the skirting board as I went down.

"Yes, something like that I guess?" she agreed as she

bent me over forwards and backwards at the waist while patting my back to assist my recovery.

"Just stop trying to be Charles Atlas all the time will you, or you'll end up in hospital and miss out on your holiday to Spain."

I had seen the said Mr. Atlas in adverts in my 'Mad' magazine comic (which explains quite a lot really), and having completed his correspondence course was forced to write to him again and request that he now send me some muscles. None arrived, and I was destined to parade the beaches of Majorca as a blindingly white five stone weakling.

Time passed by amazingly quickly, and I had weened myself down to looking at the pictures in the brochure to less than thirty times a day. Manchester Airport is only a very straight forward sixty or so miles away via the M6 and M56. Dad however, thought that to be on the safe side, we should have a dummy run to make sure we knew exactly where to turn off and locate the parking area and correct terminal etc.

We must be one of the only families in North West Britain (Nay, the world) who drove to the airport, parked up, went inside, watched planes land and take off, then went home. It was fun though, and we even spotted the same plane we would be travelling on. A Laker 1-11 jet. Good old Jim Laker, a fabulous cricketer and a damn good airline operator to boot. I think you'll find that it was Freddie Laker, bird brain. Oh yes of course, how silly of me. The founder of getting Brits abroad on the cheap.

I had a ton of questions for Dad regarding things like: How do we breathe on the plane? Can I put my head out of the window? Will I be sucked down the loo when I flush it? Will we be able to hear ourselves think over the noise of the turbines? Can I drive the plane for a bit?

He put up with some of my more sensible questions for a while before admitting that he didn't really know. He then told me to stop being silly. Can't help it Dad, I'm excited, and going on holiday to Spain. Not today like, but in two weeks' time.

The night before we travelled, I can remember Mum ironing like billy-o to get the last of our uncool outfits perfectly pressed. I have no idea what I wore to travel in, but my Stingray uniform and skull Halloween mask were nowhere to be seen in my junior suitcase. I think Mum hid them on the top of the wardrobes in their bedroom, and gave me some cock and bull story about having no idea where they were.

Then I shall have no choice but to purchase a Sombrero and Poncho as soon as we hit the sunny Mediterranean. For some reason I had confused Spain with the Wild West, and harboured an odd desire to dress up as a Mexican Bandit.

It was still daylight when I went to bed at ten o'clock the night before our big adventure, and prior to climbing into bed, I took two of my finest six shooters out of the toy cupboard and put them in their holsters. I wrapped the belt neatly around them and lay them next to my outfit for the morning. There could be things that required shooting, not just at the airport and on the plane, but on the plains in Spain, despite all the rain. Besides, what Mexican Bandit would be seen without his pistols in a hostile foreign land?

"David, if you think these damn things are going on holiday with you? Then you'd better think again young man, because they aren't. We're going to Majorca, not the O.K. Corral. Now, into bed and off to sleep pronto, we're up at five in the morning, so you need a good night's kip."

146

"Suppose you're right Mum, I don't want to upset the locals by shooting them, I guess? You never know, I suppose some of them might be okay."

And with that, my crazy swirling whirlpool of a ten year old mind drifted off to sleep with me shooting at local ruffians who were hell-bent on stealing my beautiful Señorita from me as we strolled the golden sands. Had they not seen my poncho, sombrero and six shooters?!... sadly for me, yes, they had.

I was awoken from some crazy nightmare involving Spanish local people laughing and pointing in hysterics at my Mexican bandit fancy dress outfit by the landing light being switched on. It was still dark, but I could hear Mum giving Dad last minute reminders regarding the back garden gate, the immersion heater and making sure I didn't pack my six shooters when no one was looking.

A bit bleary eyed, and minus my revolvers, we finally loaded up the racing green MG Magnet with our cases, and the well-rehearsed journey to Manchester Airport was ready to roll. My levels of excitement were off the chart, although they were tempered with some gut churning anxiety about flying for the first time. What if I got air sick? Or started to panic about being sealed in a metal tube travelling at four hundred miles an hour? Or my head suddenly exploded due to the pressurisation of the cabin? Like I said, off the chart. Well I shall have to worry about that later, as I'm sure my Dad has just driven straight past our turn off.

"Err, Dad? Wasn't that our turn off?"

"Don't think so? The one I remember from the dress rehearsal had a big picture of a plane on the sign."

"Yeah, so did the one we just passed."

"Are you sure?"

Mum, Kate and I all shout yes together.

"Whoops, well we'll take the next exit and do a U-turn. Can't be far?"

Twenty two miles later and with us all crying about not going to Spain cause we missed the turn off, my old fella suddenly turns into Sterling Moss and flattens the accelerator as we head back in the right direction. His determination to either kill us all or make the flight was admirable. We arrived at the parking area with a mere three hours to spare.

"What time is our flight?"

"Twelve thirty, but I thought it best to be on the safe side."

It was twenty past nine. I knew I should have brought my guns.

Once in the airport we tried our best to pass as seasoned travellers who had done this many times before. This façade soon ended when we were turned back from passport control and instructed to go back and check our luggage in. It may have been my fault for suggesting that you give them to the baggage handlers on the tarmac just before you get on board. Despite our early faux pas, there was still no one queuing before us at check in. There was no one at check in, full stop. It didn't open for another hour. It may well have been my fault for suggesting that all check-ins open at five a.m. and stay open all day.

We now had an hour to kill being robbed blind in the cafes, and browsing around WH Smith's looking for suitable reading material for the flight. My choices of the 'Karma Sutra', 'Lady Chatterley's lover' and a 'Playboy' magazine were hastily put back on the shelves by Mum as she told me not to be, 'bloody silly'. I was allowed a paperback copy of 'Winnie the Pooh' and the 'Beano' summer special. My suggestion that I could read Playboy secreted inside the Beano so as not to draw unwanted attention, earned me a clip round the ear. Dad contented himself with 'Reader's Digest' and 'Auto car', Mum got 'Woman's Weekly' and 'War and Peace', and Kate got 'Jackie' summer special and 'Five go bonkers in Majorca'. No, of course not, that would just be silly. There was only four of us.

After what seemed like an eternity (two hours) and with me exhausted from silently choosing who and what needed shooting, there was a call that our flight was ready to board. There was the usual surge of desperate people who wanted to be first on the plane. Well you're not first, because the pilots and crew were. We were happy with halfway down the queue, as all our nerves were jangling a little bit by now. Watching what others do is important if you don't want to make a clown of yourself. I never watch what people do, as making a clown of myself is a lifelong ambition of mine. I have however recently considered watching clowns to see if it in any way increases my levels of stupidity.

I heard the family behind us ask a member of the ground crew what that funny jangling noise was.

"It's the Hogarths' in front of you. Nerves. First time abroad etc."

Before you knew it we were buckled up in our seats and ready for take-off. My requests to go for a poo and to be allowed to experience take-off from the safety of the overhead locker were denied. I had a window seat, as per my demands, and wasn't sure now that I really fancied seeing the ground get further and further away as we sped skywards at two hundred plus miles an hour. I hastily recited the Lord's Prayer in my head, and managed a less than confident sickly smile as our jet reached the end of its taxi journey, turned sharp right on a sixpence, and rocked to a halt facing straight down the runway. I was just about to cut some terrified witty remark, when there was a sudden increase in noise like a lion roaring directly in your face. I was pinned back into my seat like a rag doll with an expression of open mouthed discombobulation. The pick-up and acceleration was way too much for an excited ten-year old to comprehend, and to be honest, there may well have been an audible outburst from my trouser seat region. Thankfully, the thrust of two Rolls Royce engines was enough to at least drown out the sound. Slowly, my sickly smile receded and I began to enjoy this mad surge of power and speed for what it was. A mad surge of power and speed. When finally the tip of the plane lifted and we left the ground, I had been left in no doubt whatsoever... this was cool.

Once airborne and cruising at thirty five thousand feet, my levels of giddy excitement increased tenfold. My first trick was to fashion a little hat out of the sick bag, and pop up out of my seat so Dad could see it. He was in stitches. I got a thick ear off Mum. The Hostess frostily replaced it, explaining that these were only to be used to vomit into. Alright, alright, keep your hat on, love, I was only trying to bag a few laughs. Leave it with me, and I'll see what I can do after I've eaten the on-board meal.

"Read your book or your summer special for a bit David will you? Just behave for goodness sake. You'll have us thrown off if you start acting daft."

"I hope they provide parachutes then Mum, it's a hell of a drop."

"Look, the food's coming around now, put your table down ready. Hopefully, this will keep you quiet for a while?"

It sure did, it was horrific. I did try to liven things up a bit by requesting red wine with my meal. Mum told me to stop being silly and said I'd have a coke. My attempts to open the little packet of crackers resulted in the near blinding of a nice man across the aisle. The refresher chew sized piece of mature cheddar I cut into thinner slices and put two of them in my mouth as dangly fangs. If only I had my Halloween skull mask now, the hilarious effect would have been complete.

"David! Will you please stop acting daft and playing with your food?"

Well anything was better than eating it. Meal complete, and with crumbs and coke all mopped up, I had urgent need of a toilet visit to post off some air logs. My Dad was assigned the job of making sure I didn't end up in the cockpit. When it was finally our turn at El Boggo (Spanish, for toilet), I slipped in and shut the tiny folding door knowing full well that Dad was standing guard outside. I was half way through my pony when my Father inexplicably pushed open the door to ask if I was okay!?

"What…?" (I thought), "I'm having a dump, Dad, close the door you donut," (I thought)." In reality, I hastily covered my genitals and mouthed, "Close the door for God's sake, I'm fine." Half the queue, and two of the cuter hostesses were cruelly treated to a full-on glimpse of me in the midst of a mid-air bowel movement. Some of them may have never recovered. Me neither. Still, at least the hostesses were smiling at me now. Or was it giggling? I convinced myself they were smiling.

When we finally got back to our seats, and my face became a paler shade of white again, my Dad collared one of the cute hostesses and asked if it would be possible for him and me to go up into the cockpit and have a chat with the Captain! I kid you not. This was the sixties, when health and safety and security was your own lookout. Terrorism back then would have been a piece of cake. Well, until they tightened the rules up a bit. A minute or two later, cutie pops was back with her giggly little smile, and a cordial invite for Dad and me to go and hang out with the pilots. My cheek and swagger restored, we strolled down the aisle to the front, and were duly ushered into the business end of the plane. Dad issued my instructions on entry.

"Behave yourself sunny Jim, and don't touch anything, or your Mum will murder you."

Even I, have some sense of decorum (very little, but some), and having now been introduced to the Captain and First Officer, I decided that, for the safety of all the other passengers, I would be a good little lad for a change. It was overwhelming. Not being a good little lad, the cockpit. These two cool guys were really lovely to Dad and me. We talked football, cute hostesses, everything. El Capitan (Spanish for, The Captain) pointed out landmarks of significance as we gazed out of the windscreen in complete awe of the view. Kilimanjaro, Sydney Harbour Bridge, Saturn. He was either pulling our legs, testing our northerners' grasp of geography, or drunk. He was pulling our legs (thankfully). What happened next, made my holiday. The Captain asked me, in a moment of mind-bending irresponsibility, if I would like to bank the plane as we were about to change course slightly. I'm not messing. I'm not sure who was more terrified, me, or Dad?... Dad, without a doubt. There was a biggish dial in the middle of the centre console with an arrow pointing straight ahead. He told me to turn it very gently and very slowly to the left until he said to stop. I think I heard Dad fart at this point, which did ruin the moment somewhat. I looked up at him for encouragement and was a little disturbed to see an expression of impending doom and sheer disbelieving terror written all over his face.

Undeterred, I started to turn the dial slowly and gently, two words that were quite unfamiliar to my crash bang wallop of a mind. As I turned, I felt the plane slowly start to bank over to the left.

"Keep going," my Co-pilot with the stripes and fancy hat said. I was doing it! I was flying a commercial passenger airliner all by myself. All of a sudden all the other dials, switches, levers and buttons became unbearably attractive! And what's this? This lever here marked 'Passenger Ejector Release Lever' (Never ever use, ever). It's so lovely, so red, so alluring... perhaps if I just pull it a little bit...

"David! David!? Okay you can stop now." said the kindly Captain as he forcibly prised my reluctant hand off the dial quite urgently.

"That was brilliant, well done, and thanks for coming up to see us. Best get back to your seats now as we'll be landing soon. Once we get back on course that is."

An hour and a half later, and finally back in Spanish air space, it was buckle up and trays locked away time, we're about to start our final approach into Palma, Majorca.

I had to shield my eyes quite heavily, as looking out through my window, I could see what appeared to be sunshine. It looked ferociously hot, and my flesh agreed. I would require several thick coatings of sun tan lotion to prevent spontaneous combustion at the first contact with the unfiltered sunlight.

More urgently, I was praying that Captain Marvel and

his pal were sufficiently sober to get us down onto the runway in one piece. We were given a boiled sweet to help with the agonising pain and pressure in our ear drums. It served no other purpose than a distraction, until I almost choked on it, which seemed to help my ear drum trauma. It equalised the pressure with my windpipe being blocked, I guess? Then I went blind. Oh, smashing, it's a right old laugh this flying malarkey, I thought, as Mum whacked my back, dislodged my sweet, and helped restore my swirling vision. With a final bump that would suggest our pilots had a couple of lagers with lunch, we were on terra firma at last.

"Ladies and gentlemen, welcome to Palma International Airport. Thank you for flying with us today. We hope you enjoy your stay here on the beautiful island of Majorca, and we look forward to taking care of you again sometime very soon. The local temperature here in Palma is currently hotter than the sun, and your nearest burns treatment centre is at Palma International Hospital which specialises in the care of gormless partially cremated British tourists, who show a total disregard for the flesh incinerating capabilities of the Mediterranean sun. On behalf of the crew, myself and the first officer, thanks again for flying Laker Airways, and if you can? Sit in the shade a bit. The sun in Spain, deals mainly in zee pain."

My giggly hostess friends were all smiles as we got to the aircraft door to disembark. One ruffled my hair and said, "You're funny." Oh cheers, thanks very much. Why? Because you saw me and Mr. Winky with my strides down having a pony. Toilet humour, eh?

Mum refused to let me stay and chat with her a bit more which was a real shame. The hair ruffle I felt was a sure sign of a future romantic relationship? Maybe not. As we emerged into the daylight at the top of the aircraft steps I heard Dad swearing at the heat again.

He was spot on. It was like the same experience you get when you open the oven door to check on a half roasted Sunday lunch, and your face is enveloped in flesh melting waves of aromatic thermodynamics.

By the time we reached baggage reclaim, my broken heart had mended, and I had stopped crying enough to be able to help lift our luggage off the carousel. We were all exhausted and dripping wet with sweat from the fifty yard walk to the terminal building. After several over enthusiastic retrievals of other peoples' cases, and Mum saying,

"David, will you just stand over there, we'll get them." We finally had all the right baggage and headed for the exit to look for our Rep. The building was swarming with very smiley very tanned people, trying to round up the white lost sheep that belonged to them specifically.

Finally, we spotted the Laker holidays representative, and I immediately fell in love again. I could see this was going to be a difficult vacation that may inflict irreparable damage to my already badly bruised heart. She was young, slim, and tanned with a dazzling smile, and smelled fantastic. Oh yes, I never left her side, and was close enough to be treated to a waft of her foreign deodorant every time she waved at more of the dim sheep milling around with Laker luggage labels.

With our party all accounted for, we followed her out to the waiting line of coaches. I followed her more closely than most, and after nearly tripping her up a couple of times, I was yanked back a few feet by Mum who was frowning and shaking her head at me.

"Take it easy Casanova, she's a bit old for you, sunny

Jim".

Ha, age is but a number, dear Mother, I thought, as I pretended not to have any idea what she was on about. I would have to play it sneaky now, and show no interest in Francesca whatsoever. At least until Mum wasn't looking that is. Oh I'm watching young man, there are very few occasions when I haven't got an eye on you. Damn clever these Mums you know?

Our coach was way back in the line, and Dad was mumbling, "Typical, couldn't be right at the front, could it? No of course not, not in this heat, oh no. I mean how far back does this damn line stretch, for Christ's sake?"

Thankfully, Francesca suddenly caught up with us and declared that ours was the next coach along. We were then head counted again, and introduced to our wonderful driver, Jose. Jose, according to Francesca, was the finest driver on the island. He certainly looked like he was the biggest and sweatiest.

Jose, was as wide as he was tall, and judging from the saturated dark patches on his pale blue short sleeved shirt, had decided that antiperspirant was not for him... no way, Jose. He was clearly of the same opinion regarding deodorant. The whiff from the heat haze that surrounded him would have blinded a young buffalo. He wouldn't have got a kick in a stampede, the pong was that strong. He wasn't for smiling either. After Francesca had bigged him up with her lovely, cheery smiley introduction, he remained completely inanimate and expressionless. I whispered to Dad I thought he might be dead. It would have helped to explain the smell at least. His head suddenly turned in my direction. He had mirrored sunglasses on, so I can't be sure if I was getting the evil eye or not, but if I was a betting man?

Apart from opening the luggage flaps on the side of the coach, he did little else. Other than sweat of course. I tried my best to engage with him by asking, and pointing, "In here, Jose?", as I struggled to lift my junior suitcase off the melting tarmac. I am almost certain he nodded his head a tiny fraction. Jose was going to be a real barrel of laughs, I could tell. I reassured myself that him being a big fat sweaty rude Spanish coach driver, was just an act. It wasn't. He couldn't drive, either!

When he eventually managed to wedge himself in behind the wheel, he immediately had to squeeze himself out again to get out and adjust the wing mirror that one of the other finest drivers on the island had whacked as he went past.

Jose meant business now, as he fired up the beast and began manoeuvres to get us out of the coach queue. How do I know he meant business? Because he had a matchstick in the corner of his mouth, and was wearing a baseball cap. From where we were sitting, it looked like he was trying to unscrew and wrench the steering wheel out of its housing. What this burst of fevered activity would do to his sweat glands was anyone's guess. My guess, was that if he didn't drink something soon, he would die of dehydration. After shunting the coach behind, twice, and scraping the wall as we pulled out, our adventure with Majorca's premier coach driver was truly up and running.

All the windows were wide open, which meant that now we were moving, boiling hot air was streaming in and baking us all alive in our seats. Jose was comforted by a little fan on the dashboard, and a litre bottle of water that he kept taking huge gulps from, thank goodness. He made no attempt to deploy the air conditioning as according to Jose it was, "Beet chilli to dye, yez?" My God! he does speak after all. His driving was erratic, aggressive and unpredictable, and there were some terrifyingly hairy moments on some of the higher coastal road bends. He showed a flagrant disregard for highway laws and other road users, blasted his horn, shook his fist out of the window, and screamed what I presume were obscenities in Spanish at everyone else who went past in the other direction. None of this was doing anything to allay my fears that Jose, was in fact, as mad as a carrot.

To distract myself from our driver's lunacy, I had positioned myself strategically so I could see Francesca, her brown legs and her clipboard and microphone. I began to wonder where we would live, and how many kids we would have. Mum stopped me right in my tracks and told me to stop staring at her and sit back in my seat properly.

"Look out of the damn window David, will you, and stop gawping at Francesca, you'll frighten her." Oh cheers Mum, thanks. She did have a point though. I had already drawn a couple of frowns from her, and it was only a matter of time before she would accompany it with a shake of her head as well. It was hard work being a horny ten year old. You have no idea of protocol at that age, so you just stare and make inappropriate comments to people directly. Things like,

"Francesca? Do you wear underwear in summer in Spain? Or is it too hot?"

The contrast of childlike innocence, and my desire for the answer to be 'No', was confusing to say the least.

"Ha ha." she laughed nervously, showing me her gorgeous teeth,

"Of course we do. It is very warm here in summer, but you should always wear underwear. Clean underwear of course. Why do you ask?"

"Well, to cut a long story short, I'm crackers, and think you're gorgeous, but I can't see the line of your knickers under your pretty little pale yellow cotton dress."

After an awkward silence that seemed to last forever, Francesca clicked on her microphone and began commentating on areas of local interest for people to gaze at through the coach windows.

"Will you behave, David!? What kind of a question is that to be asking at ten years old? And what business is it of yours anyway whether she's got any knickers on or not?"

"She hasn't got any underpants on Mum! I mean, what kind of country is this? Oh… and I think I'm in love with her."

"I'll give you 'in love with her' in a minute, young man. You're ten, and she's in her twenties for god's sake. Read your summer special, or look out of the window, but leave the poor girl alone."

I spent the rest of the journey to our hotel watching her via the reflection in my window. I could keep an eye on Francesca without even looking at her. I did keep laughing like a maniac at every mildly amusing quip she made on the mic. It may get me back in her good books if I show appreciation of her hilarious running commentary regarding some of the local area hot spots. They were all hot spots, it was about ninety six degrees in the shade.

When we eventually arrived at our hotel, Jose was about half the man he used to be, and there was a huge puddle under his seat. I hope it was just sweat. He'd lost so much weight on the forty minute drive that he was now fit enough to help us get our cases off the coach. Well, mine. It was the smallest after all.

"Enjoy your 'oliday Senor." said Jose, as he handed me my luggage.

"I will, Jose, thank you, and thanks for somehow getting us here in one piece."

"No problem, boss, eez my job, yez? Watch out for all zee pretty ladies Senor, eh?" which he accompanied with a sly smile and a wink.

"I will indeed Jose, eez my job, no?"

We both had a chuckle, and I decided that, despite smelling like an unkempt thirty year old donkey with a perspiration disorder, Jose was okay. He was now my newly appointed unofficial best pal and unsung local hero.

I later discovered there was a legendary local song about Jose, the finest driver in the land, and was forced to adjust my opinion as a result.

"Now." said Francesca, "Would you like to follow me into reception, and we can get you all booked in to your rooms?"

Does a bear dump in the woods? I thought to myself. Yes of course we'd like to follow you into reception. I'd like to follow you around for the rest of my life, but I have a feeling Mum may have other ideas. Like, suggesting I wear my armbands in the pool for instance, while Francesca was talking to other guests within earshot, ten feet away. I whizzed my armbands over the hotel wall onto some scrubland. Sadly, as they were fluorescent orange, Mum spotted them, and sent Dad to fetch them.

"How did they end up over there David? You didn't fling them over there did you?"

"I most certainly did not, thank you very much. I think a Coyote took a fancy to them Mum. They're attracted to bright orange apparently."

I just got the look on this occasion, the one that says, "You lying hound." Well, you know what they say about sleeping dogs don't you?

"We're in Majorca, David, not Yellowstone Park."

"Okay Boo-boo, well it looked like a Coyote, it was probably just a local stray dog that fancied a swim to cool off."

For now though, we needed to do as we were told, and follow the lovely Francesca into reception and discover what delights our rooms had in store for us. Besides ants, that is.

There weren't many people before us to check in, but we were about to be introduced to the Spanish way of doing things. Slowly. I mean, we were introduced quickly to how slowly they did things. If they had introduced us slowly to how slowly they did things, then it would have slowed things down a lot more than it did, and we would have been there a lot longer.

Slowly it dawned on us that this wasn't going to happen quickly, checking in that is, and very quickly, we realised that it was going to be a really long, slow process.

I may have digressed a little here, but I'm sure you get the gist of things? When it was our turn at the reception desk, I fell in love again for the second time in two hours. Margarita, the receptionist (not the tequila based cocktail), was more tanned than a sun worshipper who had failed to apply sun screen ever, had teeth whiter than Tin Tin's dog Snowy, and was blessed with bone crunchingly good looks, dark hair, brown eyes, and glossy lips.

I may well have murmured, "Hubba-hubba" under my breath at this point. I was rewarded with a half glare, half smile from Margarita, and a sharp tug on the sleeve of my T-shirt from Mum. My verbal admiration of our check-in cutie did nothing to speed up the handing over of our keys. I forgave her though as it meant I could gawp at her for a bit longer. How I was going to juggle two Spanish beauties for an entire week was beyond me, as indeed, are most things.

Our rooms were up on the ninety third floor, and we joined the queue for the space shuttle to take us up there. No, of course not, that would be silly. We were on the fourth floor overlooking the pool at the rear of the building. Me and Kate in a twin, and Ma and Pa in a double room next door. Our room had the highest population of ants ever recorded anywhere on planet Earth. The colony had some fifty billion members. I know this for a fact, as I counted them all the day I was confined to the room with sunburn and heatstroke. I may have been delirious, so my numbers could be a bit out.

It took us a while to get up to the rooms, as each time the lift doors opened at ground floor it was still crammed full with people who had failed to alight due to congestion. It said, lift capacity, six people. I counted nine as the doors closed again and the arguing continued in an upward direction. A young couple at the back didn't seem to notice, and just carried on snogging, oblivious to everything. I imagined that would be how I would look kissing Francesca or Margarita, or both. I also imagined that I'd have to be stood on a chair to reach them.

Once in our rooms, Kate and I were instructed to unpack our cases and put everything into the drawers and wardrobes nice and neatly. I lifted all of my stuff out in one go, and plonked it in the top drawer. Minimum effort, no need for over complication, job done. Kate tutted at me, pulled a face, and shook her head. Oh don't worry yourself, this is the default response I get from just about everyone, even to this very day.

I wrenched out my swimwear from the bottom of the little pile and turned my back on Kate, before whizzing my pants off and pulling my trunks on. She was spared a glimpse of the little fella due to my lightning speed and high levels of sneakiness. It was about three in the afternoon but still hot enough to boil a monkey's bum. I would have to ensure I was well coated in sun protection as I had no plans to be hospitalised when there was so much romance in the air. I went out on to our balcony while I waited for slow coach to get her costume on and do whatever it is thirteen year old girlies do? When I looked down onto the pool area, I could not believe my 'three cherries fruit machine jackpot' eyes. Lying around the pool in pleasantly sufficient numbers were fully formed female persons with nothing covering the upper parts of their anatomies.

"Hurry up Kate, will you? The pool looks fantastic, and there are some free sunbeds at the moment." Now then, which of those bronzed bathing beauties shall we plonk ourselves next to I wonder? I also wonder if I will be able to keep my jaw shut and not gawp unblinkingly at them for hours on end. No, was the answer to that one.

As we emerge into the lovely Spanish afternoon sunshine, I realise that sun screen alone will not prevent my pallid English flesh from crisping up and falling off within minutes. Heat was bouncing off just about every surface possible, and I considered a quick dash to the local Supermacado (Spanish for, 'Spar shop') for a large tub of goose fat, for some thicker protection. On our actual first visit to the Supermacado, and after several exhausting minutes trying to impersonate a fat goose, Mum told me to curtail my pointless charade as the assistant was becoming frightened, and she didn't think they would have any anyway. Once we calmed the shop assistant down and stopped her crying, we got some chocolate fingers and tea bags for in our rooms. Our attempt to buy milk of any description, failed. We bought a carton of something that had the picture of a cow on, but the liquid inside had never seen a cow, let alone emerge from its richly nourished udders. There were udders to choose from, but we didn't bother. What?! I am only ten.

Meanwhile back at the pool, we get ourselves settled with four sun beds pleasantly close to some half naked women that Mum didn't seem to notice, but Dad did. Well done Pops, nice work. I get the wink and sly grin from Dad as we're opening our towels out and getting comfy.

"This seems like a good spot. Not too far from the bar, and nice and close to the pool for a dip if you get a bit too warm."

And surrounded by bare breasted stunners, I was going to add, but thought that it might blow Dad's cover, so resisted. Kate and Mum were too busy slapping lotion on to notice Dad and I mouthing hello and smiling at our new poolside neighbours. None of them responded, as they were asleep with sunglasses on. Still, you have to be pleasant and try, at least. We weren't the only blindingly white people around the pool either. There were a couple of other families who had also clearly been imprisoned and kept away from daylight for many years.

Enough of this boring observation I thought, and before Mum could even get my armbands out of the straw beach bag, I scurried across the paving and leapt into the deep end taking the form of a small ape shaped bomb. The reason I scurried as opposed to stroll nonchalantly, was because my feet had caught fire as soon as they were planted on the white hot paving. I came up gasping for air and laughing falsely, not because the pool was cold, but because it would be a miracle if I were ever to be able to walk normally again.

As I splashed around wildly with all the grace of a severely burned water monkey child, some of the poolside beauties sat up to see what all the commotion was about. This then gave me a front on view of a host of dangling bosoms that meant I would have to remain in the pool until the little guy had calmed down a bit. Still, it gave the incinerated soles of my feet a chance to cool off. Despite Mum standing on the side of the pool waving my armbands at me, I continued to glide effortlessly up and down and pretended I couldn't see or hear her. I could swim, but my style more resembled the tussle between a determined hungry shark, and an equally determined not to be eaten victim. Entertaining and flamboyant yes, but messy. To further prove my aquatic prowess I decided to impress the galleries by swimming the entire length of the pool underwater. I surfaced after ten metres, gulping for air noisily, and rubbing my chlorinated eyeballs as I had decided to open them down below to see where I was going.

This was going really well. I was now partially blind with glowing red eyes, and only able to hobble short distances on my blackened stumps for feet. My final idiotic accomplishment for the afternoon was to attempt a dive into the pool for the very first time ever. Hey, I was ten, a seasoned swimmer, and with some kneeling dives as practice back home, what could possibly go wrong. Quite a bit as it turned out.

With Mum watching like a hawk, and her verbal warning of,

"Just be careful David, you haven't done much diving before, just take it easy, young man", ringing in my ears, I hobbled clumsily to a spot down near the deep end, and mustered up some uncertain courage ready to take the plunge. Bizarrely, I stretched my arms out wide in readiness, like a high board specialist, then inhaled massively to expand my tiny chest to its full capacity. If people weren't watching before, then they sure were now. This was going to be something special. Oh boy, it was special alright. I bent at the knees for what seemed like forever as the water now looked a lot further away than I remembered during kneeling dives. As my levels of doubt reached fever pitch, I decided it was now, or never. With a flurry of complicated limb spasms, I became airborne due to slippage on the poolside tiles, and despite my efforts in mid-air to re-calibrate, I came down flat and almost horizontal onto the unforgiving surface of the water. There was a sound that resembled a clap of thunder overhead, and my winded and lifeless body drifted embarrassingly out into the centre of the pool for all to see. As I came to, with Dad encouraging me to breathe, and a crowd peering down at me, I spotted Francesca's happy smiling face, which, as my focus improved, turned out to be a head shaking frown. The other small child that I landed on, who was innocently swimming past at the time, also made a full recovery. Physically at least. I also seem to remember hearing Mum's voice threatening to murder me if I didn't stop acting daft.

With partially sunburnt flesh, crippled incinerated feet, and a red chest from water impact injuries, I and my sister retired to our room with instructions to be ready to go down for dinner at half past six. This was mainly because Dad was starving and he had rightly guessed that the dining room would be quieter at that time. He was spot on. Most people were still lying around the pool fast asleep. Unconscious, in some cases, from wine and beer over indulgence. There was a smattering of other British family groups in there who were also on UK eating times. There was all the usual half smiling and mouthing hellos nonsense as you passed by other diners to get to your table. Dad stopped to chat to one chap who seemed friendly. I heard Dad curse the heat. The other guy replied in some strange sounding dialect that meant we had no idea what had been said. Dad nodded and laughed as if he understood and we moved along quickly to our allotted table. "What did he say?" Dad asked. "Something about having his adenoids and appendix out, I think?" was my best offer. Mum and Kate just shook their heads bewildered. Turned out they were Scottish, and he was talking about his football team, Hamilton Academicals.

"David thought you were talking about having your adenoids and appendix out." Dad confessed kindly for me at the bar later.

"Oh he did, did he? The cheeky wee monkey."

I got that bit alright, but I was still going to have to buy a Scottish translation book if we were to converse any further during the week. They were a good laugh though, and the elder of their two sons I had noticed had his eye keenly on Kate most of the time. Some "You've got a boyfriend!" taunts would be flying her way once we got back to our room later.

Back at the dining table, we awaited the arrival of some waiting staff, who would, we hoped, come and wait on us, if we waited patiently, and waited to see what delights the evening menu had to offer. I don't think they had arrived for work yet, as we sat for ages with just the occasional slight opening of the kitchen swing door to reveal a puzzled looking kitchen porter. At about seven o'clock an unshaven frenzied chap appeared, still doing his shirt up, and adjusting his black bow tie as he scooted around tossing menu cards onto the three tables where there were starving British holidaymakers. As he went sprinting past, I had to wonder if he was related to Jose the coach driver, as he seemed to be afflicted with the very same aroma.

None of the menu was in English (What is wrong with these Spaniards?), and we had to make uneducated guesses at what would be edible from the complicated jumble of ineligible letters, squiggles and accents. I spotted that melon could be one of the starters, and there was a Gestapo soup, that sounded a bit iffy. Through sign language and animal impersonations (there was no goose on tonight), we did our stiff upper lip best to place our order in the most dignified way possible. I think the other two families thought we were trying to teach our waiter the words to 'Old MacDonald's Farm'.

My melon was as hard as rocks, and Dad sent his Gestapo soup back because it was stone cold. Mum said she thought that's how it was supposed to be. God help us all. The main course paella, had dead prawns in it that were still in full armour coating, and their tasty sweet flesh was nigh on impossible to extract without ending up covered in scales and prawn juice. Despite vigorous scrubbing, my fingers stunk of fish for the entire week.

Exhausted from day one of our Spanish adventure, we retired to bed at about ten o'clock. We were on holiday so we were going to cut loose. Well, maybe tomorrow. Once Kate and I had cleared our beds of ants, we got under the single white sheets for a good night's rest. This was the late sixties, and air conditioning was something yet to be embraced in hotel bedrooms in Spain. As it was still a hundred degrees, even now it was dark, we opened our balcony door to let some refreshing warm air in to cool us down. There was the enchanting sounds of crickets too. They all seemed to be gathered in the trees and garden areas right outside our window. This increasing crescendo of frantic leg rubbing got louder by the minute and was only drowned out by the sound of rowdy drunk people throwing each other in the pool. This went on way beyond midnight, so, boiling hot, covered in ants, and unable to nod off due to crickets and noisy hooligans arguing with the hotel night staff, I stared at the ceiling and wondered just how my sister had managed to fall asleep with no problem at all. I shall ask her in the morning before we go to the beach. Now, what track is this that's playing on the juke box in the bar? Oh yes, of course, 'Mama told me not to come'... again.

It turned out, my sister's ears had filled up with ants, and she had been unable to hear anything once they had nestled in and settled down for the evening. I was determined to rid our room of these pesky intruders and so later in the day on our return from the beach I was going to investigate. I suspected there was going to have to be a whole lot of stamping to be done, and with my feet still throbbing from a good toasting on the pool tiles earlier, I needed to figure out how else I could commit mass murder on an industrial scale without crippling myself.

Down on the beach we found a suitable spot to set up camp, and readied ourselves to tackle the delights of the Mediterranean Sea. Mum and Dad were happy to let Kate and I have first dibs on a swim. They would remain in camp and keep guard of our valuables (a straw bag, some towels and sun tan lotion) in case there were any local Banditos (Mexican, for Bandits) looking to add to their accessories and towel collections. My sister Kate was a really good swimmer, but she was a serious swimmer who would swim up and down for about fifteen minutes, then go back to lazing in the sun. I was someone who preferred to stay in longer and just muck about. I would swim a bit, then sit in the shallows and observe topless ladies walk in up to their waist and just stand there with mind bogglingly large boobs and nipples. I would eventually tire of this and then swim under water and open my eyes to check their legs out. Forgetting of course that it was salt water and near blinding myself again.

With Kate watching our towel ensemble, Mum and Dad ventured in together, tip toeing further out holding hands of course. Mum quizzed me on the way past, "I hope you're behaving yourself, young man? Go and sit with your sister and keep her company while we have a quick dip, there's a good lad."

"Okay. Don't go out too far folks, I saw some fins out there before."

"Ha ha, very funny… you didn't, did you?"

"Could have been Dolphins I suppose?"

"Pay no attention to him, he's just pulling your leg." Dad reassured Mum.

"Is that why you're sitting in the shallows? You big Mary Ellen" he added.

I gave Dad a sarcastic friendly grin and wink, and nodded at a beach babe behind him while Mum wasn't looking. He had a crafty glance and turned back to me shaking his head with a thumbs up.

I had a quick mental check that my little man was in neutral, and as he was, I was able to rise from the waves like a small ten year old nutcase on holiday, and loving it.

My parents drifted out to sea, and were eaten by sharks. No of course not, that would be ridiculous. They did however encounter some other terrors of the deep. When I say deep, I mean five foot down on the rocks around the edge of the bay. They stopped for a quick breather and stood on the rocks before swimming back to shore. As they walked back up the beach Dad was grimacing and hobbling a bit, and Mum was half supporting him with her arm around his waist.

"Told you there were sharks out there."

"Not sharks, you cheeky monkey barnacles."

As Kate and I had fits of the giggles together, Dad tried to see what damage had been inflicted to the soles of his feet. With mine scalded black, and Dad's riddled with tiny black sea urchins, we would now be pitied by all who saw us trying to walk bow-legged on the edges of our feet. Their only conclusions could be, that the male side of the Hogarth ancestry had fallen foul of Rickets at some point in history.

It was decided that we would be far safer around the pool back at the hotel. First though, we were going to try a café just off the beach for a late lunch. It was a late lunch because we had realised that going in for dinner at the hotel at six thirty was boring, and they didn't serve you till half past seven anyway.

The food at the café was far better than at the hotel, and after polishing off chicken and chips and a whopper of an ice cream, I knew I had enough fuel in the engine to make it until the early evening. Dad and I hobbled back to the hotel on the edges of our mutilated feet, with passers-by either smiling at our funny antics, or others grimacing in sympathy at our hideous afflictions. Mum and Kate walked on ahead, and did their best to disown us and our exaggerated silly walks.

Back at reception, Mum tried her best to ask for a scalpel, tweezers, cotton wool, bandages and antiseptic cream. My goose impression did nothing to help, and earned me a clip around the ear for being silly.

We adjourned to our rooms for repair work on our mangled feet, and for a siesta. A short nap in the latter afternoon favoured by lazy Spanish people who use the heat as an excuse to skive off work for a bit. I slept for three hours, and was only awoken a couple of times by my Father's bloodcurdling screams as my Mum dug out the deepest of the tiny black aliens embedded in his flesh. By the evening time, Dad and I were almost walking normally again thanks to Mum's nursing skills, and no longer resembled mindless chimps larking about for laughs. Actually despite now being fully upright again, we were still larking around like mindless apes. Especially when the wine decanter was passed around to see how far from your face you could hold it and not spill any while pouring it down your throat. I managed half a decanter before Mum snatched it off me.

"What are you doing? Give me that, you idiot, it's wine David, not coca cola for God's sake."

"Tastes good though Mum… and has a rather arrogant bouquet too."

"I'll arrogant bouquet you, you'll be drunk for days you clown, glugging that much down."

I must admit I did feel a bit giddy after my introduction to the delights of cheap Spanish house wine. So much so that I enjoyed a mad impromptu little dance to 'I saw her standing there' when it came blasting out of the juke box. My half dance/goose impression was accompanied by air guitar solos and mouthed lyrics with a pretend mic that earned me muted applause from other drunk guests, but mostly frowns and shaking heads from the majority. Once the alcohol buzz wore off, I was exhausted, and my feet were killing me again.

By the middle of the week, we had become accustomed to the Spanish food and Spanish tummy. I didn't really notice much difference to my English tummy to be honest. We had hit the beach most days and endured no further barnacle or shark disasters. The café was a regular visit at two o'clock for a late full lunch, they even put whipped cream on your ice cream sundae, lovely.

There was a coach trip into Palma that we went on two days prior to coming home. I had a pretty long list of things to buy to be able to prove beyond any doubt that I had indeed been on holiday to Spain. Top of the list was a Sombrero. I had not seen a single person wearing one locally, but was convinced that there would be plenty of occasions back home where it would be stupid not to wear it. That was how I convinced Mum it was really needed. Once we had found a shop that had one small enough to fit my little chimp's head, I got the go ahead from Mum with her unconvincing endorsement that I wouldn't wear it in a month of Sundays. I tried to wear it to church the first Sunday we got home only to have it rudely snatched off my head and told,

"You aren't going to church in that, young man, take it off." My decision to try, had been influenced by the month of Sunday's challenge.

As Mum forked out whatever it cost to the giggling shop assistant, I couldn't help wondering what a truly fabulous, fantastic loving Mum I had. Gullible at times yes, but awesome in every sense of the word. For the record, it was of platted straw design with the typical rounded witch's hat pointy bit (The hat, not my Mum). There was a black silk trim on the upturned brim that had orange, yellow and green zig-zags on to indicate Mexican bandit impudence and hostility toward cowardly villagers. As usual Mum was spot on with her predication that I'd never wear it once I was back in Blackpool. I did wear it once, and that was to show my pal John. He didn't stop laughing for about an hour. It then found its way on to the top of my wardrobe. Every morning when I woke up I could see it, a wonderful reminder of my first fabulous holiday abroad. More importantly it reminded me of a Mum who seemed like she would do anything to make her nutcase of a little lad happy. Even if it meant buying me a ridiculous hat that I would never wear.

If you need any further proof of my Mum's unconditional love, wait till you see the rest of my souvenir purchases that I insisted I needed badly. In order of insanity on an increasing scale, a bullfight poster, castanets, maracas, a small model of a bull with two spears sticking out of its back, and a small presentation box with two replica miniature spears in. I looked like I had been to the bullfight and loved it so much, that I had decided to join the band. The castanets were impossible to master to the standard I desired from one go, and were therefore never picked up again. The maracas were so easy to master, that I was bored with them after a few shakes, and they met with a similar fate. I had pictures in my head of me playing the maracas with my sombrero on in my bedroom at home like some frustrated leader of a yet to be formed Mariachi band. The bull model was too disturbing for me to look at ever again after I witnessed a quick glimpse of a real bullfight as we walked past a tapas bar full of toothless old Spanish men in beer stained grey trousers and white vests watching one on TV. Despite their happy and enthusiastic cheering, the whole spectacle was gut wrenchingly cruel and grotesque. I shouted, "Come on bully," as we passed by, and it seemed I was his only fan. The two replica spears were thrown regularly at Action Man while he was swinging on my bedroom light switch cord. They didn't stick in if they hit him, but they did gouge out chunks of wallpaper that earned me the usual death threats and a thick ear. My bullfight poster did get a chance up on the wall because the depiction was of a skilled matador avoiding contact with bully beef by means of magical cape wielding. The amount of claret in the picture had been sensitively reduced to ensure more sales to naïve British tourists. I did like my poster, despite it featuring the legendary El Cordobes who slaughtered thousands of bulls during his career. That will have been some stampede that awaited him when he finally popped his clogs. I have pretty odd nightmares of my own from time to time, but nothing compared to what would be in store for him. Unlike Jose, he would be guaranteed to get a kick during stampede season.

So there is a fine example of just why sons love their Mums. Their ability to ignore all rationality when it comes to wasting money on useless items that connect to something far more important and special... memories. Your own little movie playback system that fills you with joy and warmth on cold dark windy winter's nights. All thanks to a Mother's love for a son, who was, and still is, as daft as a brush.

Our holiday almost at an end, and with skin that looked a lot healthier than when we arrived, it was time to check out and wait for the cheerfully pungent Jose to arrive with the coach. My romances with Francesca and Margarita never had a chance to develop, largely due to them being wrapped around handsome Spanish chaps who were much more appropriately aged. Damn my junior cheeky monkey

nutcase status. They did smile and ruffle my hair though…
oh, and frown and shake their heads a bit too. My attempts
to rid our bedroom of the entire planet's ant population
ended with my obligatory thick ear. I took some powdered
bleach off the cleaner's trolley and doused them liberally
with it. They just seemed to walk through it, eat it, and got
bigger. Our earlier foot injuries had all but healed, and
apart from an ear infection, diarrhoea, and partial
blindness from swimming underwater with my eyes open,
I was good to go… home.

Dad did his best on the journey back to the airport to
cheer me up with stories of a new upcoming season at
Blackpool F.C., but as anyone who has seen Blackpool
F.C. play will confirm, he was just making matters worse.
I jest, we loved going to games together, and the team of
that era held some spellbinding talent that would have
fetched millions in today's transfer market. Alan Suddick
and Tony Green to name but two. Mum and Kate were
more interested in staying home and watching 'The
Forsythe Saga' and 'The First Churchill's' on telly. They
were boring historical romantic dramas, and I can't
remember any goals being scored in any of the episodes I
watched.

Our flight back home thankfully excluded everyone
watching me on the toilet, and I spent the entire flight
daydreaming about my two failed romantic encounters.
Not a lot has changed really, to this very day. I cheered
myself up by thinking about my wonderful tourist
souvenirs, and pictured myself leaning against the bar at
the next school disco in my sombrero whilst jiggling my
maracas. This could not fail to impress the ladies… surely?
I would have to put my castanets in my gun holsters though,
as I had yet to master the technique of getting them to

make an agreeable sound. My one and only attempt to tame them, sounded like someone throwing a bucket full of wooden blocks down a stone staircase. My mind did occasionally slip into bullfight mode, where it was met by horrific images of beautiful animals being slaughtered by warped humans... for fun, and entertainment! Give me Tommy Cooper and Morecambe and Wise, any day.

I was even considering surgically removing the two spears out of my souvenir bull's back and putting sticking plasters on the holes and felt tipping them black. I was also considering using my two boxed mini spears on Action Man in a horrific fashion, so as to balance the books a bit. A voice did however whisper,

"Two wrongs don't make a right now, do they?"

"No, and one swallow doesn't mean it's summer either, but I hate to see bullying in the bull ring. Even if he was two thousand pounds with great flesh tearing horns."

21. LIFE'S LITTLE SECRET

So many wonderful memories have returned to me after the death of my Mum, it's as if she is encouraging me to recall them.

Just before her health began to deteriorate, I came back to Blackpool after having hip surgery, which had cut short a career in green keeping. I felt drawn back to Blackpool because I felt there was something not quite right with her, and despite having no job to come back to, I left a position in Bristol and headed back to the North West.

I was at a real lose end, and some of my pals had suggested I drive a taxi whilst looking for something more permanent. I agreed that if I bumped into a friend of my sister who I knew used to drive a cab, I would make enquiries.

Here is one of the first very odd coincidences. The day after deciding this, I pulled in at a petrol station I rarely use, and seconds later at the pump next to me arrives Kath (my sister's friend). I hadn't seen her for probably ten years and didn't even know if she still drove a taxi. I had no idea at this point that Kath was very spiritual and was quite popular for tarot readings. She was indeed still involved with a cab, and as if by magic, was looking for a day driver for the vehicle she was running. Her description of the job was encouraging, and once I had taken the knowledge test and got my badge she would happily let me have a go at driving days for her. This gave me the flexibility to be able to work and keep an eye on Mum at the same time.

Over the next two or three years I started to become

more interested in the spiritual things Kath and her friends would talk about. At the same time Mum went through quite a quick descent with her health and very sadly passed away.

It hit me really hard, at a time when I had just returned to my home town and now felt very alone indeed. I started to become cynical and sceptical about everything. Possibly even paranoid about the world that surrounded me. Stuff never seemed to go my way, and I was becoming an angry little man who believed in nothing. When things got to almost the very bottom of the deep dark well, something quite extraordinary happened. I found a lifebelt and a rope to climb out of the hole I was in. The rope was my meeting with Kath. Not because of the taxi work, but the introduction to the spiritual side of things that my mind had longed for and needed for so long. The lifebelt, my Mum gave to me when I was a little boy who didn't want to read much. 'A Christmas Carol', her favourite book, was my warning and my salvation rolled into one. As I have mentioned, since her death I have been convinced she connects with me through the quick crossword clues in the newspapers. That is when she needs speedy access to prevent me from imploding of course.

One morning I was sat having a coffee on my couch when I felt a sudden urge to look to my right as something was catching my eye. What happened next I do not have an explanation for? At a spot on my curtains that I could not take my eyes off, the outline of an image began to emerge. I do not lie, and if I would have said this ten years ago to myself, I would have wet myself laughing. It was like being in a trance. Maybe I was. Becoming clearer and clearer on the curtain was an image of my Mum from a favourite photo I have of her when she was young. It got sharper and more obvious for about ten or fifteen seconds then disappeared in an instant. I kid you not, I sat there with my mouth open in shock for about five minutes. I was very warm all over and didn't know what had just happened. I genuinely worried that I was beginning to lose the plot.

I mean, I know I'm bonkers, that's a given, but this I had seen with my own doubting Thomas eyes. As if to take the mickey even further, a week or so later when I kept examining my curtains for filth or a fault in the material, a feather image appeared in a different random place on the same curtains when there was no sun to create such an illusion from outside. I regularly experience feather visits at some of the most unexpected moments. All just coincidence of course? I'm not so sure anymore. They seem to drop by and nudge me if I'm being particularly downcast or angry about something. With direct clues and pointers handily located in my daily paper, I began to wonder harder about what to do about it. I certainly started to feel a lot more enthusiastic about life again. I had always fancied a crack at writing. Mum had tried so hard to get me to read more as a little lad, and Dad had always tried to influence my musical tastes towards proper music, as he would call it. But I got what he meant. Music that has melody, rhythm and a beat. So as the process of writing this book began, I re-engaged with the music from my past and more. Tunes have come bouncing out of the ether to me waving and screaming 'Me, me, listen to me'. I have, and I have taken more time to look at lyrics and their message.

This book has become more than just the writing of a happy young lad's memories. It has revealed (to me at least) that we are all connected across time and space, and always will be. TIME. The Infinite Movement of Energy. Ask the universe to help you in any way you feel comfortable with, and you will be truly amazed by how it responds. With my growing desire to write a book bubbling, I now needed a sign to get me up and running. Where else but my one and only daily read, the 'Daily Express'. My Mum and Dad are regularly within the pages of the Express, just bursting with little gems of encouragement and advice. The 'Happy Mondays' column by Carole Ann Rice, did, one very Monday, have a lovely little piece about a writing site that seemed to be rather relevant and timely. I felt guided and sure that this was a pointer not to miss, and to act upon. I signed up to 'The Novelry' to write my novel in ninety days. The result is what you are now drifting asleep to. The site is run by a very patient and wise young lady named Louise Dean. I refer to her as Boss, and she refers to me as cheeky monkey. I like it a lot, it reminds me of the relationship I had with my Mum. Louise is a lot younger, prettier, and wiser than me, but I still like her despite all that.

When I began writing, many more strange things began to occur. Perhaps the strangest of the lot was a day when my attention was drawn very keenly to my usual port of connection, crossword clues. Look at eight down and eight across my instinct happily encouraged me. This is what was there. Emit light (5 letters) and Tales (7 letters). 'Shine' 'Stories' were the answers. I was shocked to see the words, and had another open gob moment of disbelief. At that particular time, I was feeling down and disillusioned with my writing and this gave me a much needed boost. I might also add that I had already decided the title of my book should be 'Rise and Shine Little Man'.

There are a couple of other very vivid memories of my

Mum that I feel compelled to share with you before we move back towards the humour. An example of just how loving my Mum was, and how utterly ashamed I am at how a sulky impatient male can behave.

Her dementia was starting to confuse her more and more, and she wasn't remembering anything I was telling her if we made arrangements. I had said I would pick her up one Friday afternoon and take her for fish and chips for tea. She loved fish and chips. When I called up at the flat to collect her, she wasn't there. I panicked as this was not like her even as confused as she had become. Having looked around the shops in Poulton, my last idea was to head to the chippy itself, and see if she was there. To my relief she was stood outside looking worried and very anxious. Her face lit up when she saw me walking towards her. Although relieved, I was angry she had got the plans mixed up, and had gone and got a bus to where the chip shop was a few miles away from her flat.

I realised at this point that things weren't going to improve for her, and she was beginning to slide downhill. I was afraid, angry and upset, and we barely spoke a word as we both picked unconvincingly at our chippy teas. When I finally looked up at her, there were tears in her eyes, and she said to me.

"I'm so sorry David, I've spoilt your tea, haven't I?"

It was all I could do not to burst into tears right there and then. I have hated myself every day since that moment. All that mattered to Mum, was me enjoying my tea, and I was acting like an angry selfish little arsehole who was annoyed that she had got the plans mixed up and made her own way there.

"No Mum, you haven't ruined my tea, I was just upset and worried where you were that's all." The truth was, she was disappearing piece by piece before my very eyes, and I had no idea how to stop it.

We had another cup of tea and she had me smiling again within minutes, and I had her laughing again too with more of my usual cheeky monkey nonsense.

Things did however get slowly worse, and one of the last incidents before she finally went into care, was when she phoned me one morning at a quarter to six to ask if we were going out for tea. I had written my phone number down in big figures and said for her to ring me at any time if she was confused or unsure about anything. I got up and dressed and dashed straight to the flat. She had made me something to eat. It was a chocolate muffin and some hummus. I smiled at her and made a cup of tea for us both, and we sat down and had muffins and hummus together.

I loved my Mum so very much, and God knows just how much I miss her.

22. BAD MAN AND THE ANGELS

When things were deteriorating and getting worse for me, I had another very strange encounter that seemed too bizarre and coincidental to be unplanned. But it was. I had a chance meeting with someone from my past whom I used to date. It was complicated, but we had such a strong spiritual connection that we started to see each other again. I was at a very low ebb at this point. Drinking more heavily than I would normally, and beginning to think that if this was all there was to my life, then my future looked pretty dismal.

We talked a great deal, about everything, and she even said at one point that she felt she may have been sent to save me. I was certainly heading in that direction without doubt. I struggled to come to terms with what we were doing and was constantly racked with guilt and anxiety. There was a huge amount of love between us, and there always has been. At one point when I was being particularly difficult (surprise, surprise I hear you all shout) she actually said to me, "You just don't get it David, do you?" She had had a premonition many years ago when she had seen me in my car with another girl a while after we had split up. She sensed that one day somewhere in the future, we would end up together.

I only used to see her for a few hours a week really, so we used to arrange to meet at our own special little spiritual gate that led to a meadow every night when we were apart. She said she would be waiting at the gate for me, every night. I had found my angel, and sensed that Mum was smiling down on me happy that my sun was starting to shine again.

We tried really hard to hold on and make things work, but it was like a titanic tug of war between the life she had, and being with me.

I wasn't proud of myself for what we were doing, in fact, I hated myself for being responsible for trying to tear other people apart. My sun had started to rise and I felt like life was finally starting to swing in my direction. It just didn't feel quite right though. I started to become impatient and felt my mental well-being was suffering from the constant stress and uncertainty. Very sadly, for us both I think,… I let go.

Sometimes, that is what you have got to do. Not because you want to, but because it's the right thing to do. For whatever reasons there are for this lesson, I am grateful. Sometimes, it just isn't all good. There are angels out there, and they are watching and waiting to step in and help. You only have to ask. My angels aren't done with me yet, and I hope they never will be. They have sure got their work cut out though. I hope they will stand beside me and guide me until I'm done. Love doesn't always work out how you might hope or expect, but it is still love, no matter what. You won't always have it all, because no one ever does.

But just like the cup of kindness in 'A Christmas Carol', they will give you a hearty swig of the stuff when you need it most. You only have to ask, believe, and have faith.

23. LET IT SNOW

I can remember a few very snowy winters from my childhood days. We would go nuts if there was anything like a decent covering because it didn't happen all that often in Blackpool. Snowmen and sledging, yes, but snowball fight destruction was the number one priority. Teams would be picked. Yep, me and John versus. It was never any other way. Melvin, Bowie and Richard would be sent to a spot about 30 yards away. Very key this, Bowie and Richard could only chuck about 20 yards. Melvin could throw as far as John and me, but he was on a hiding to nothing as we just ignored the other two and pounded him from two directions. If Bowie and Richard dared to come any closer into range, they would receive a barrage at a much higher velocity and have to back off again.

There was a pre-battle construction phase, which allowed enough time to make about twenty thousand snowballs. Running out of ammo mid-skirmish was not an option. You would be pummelled to pieces if you were re-loading under fire. We did get beaten the odd time JP and me, but it was rare. Very rare. Almost never. Melvin made the big mistake one time of ambushing me and stuffing handfuls of snow down my back. A twenty minute pursuit then took place with him just out of reach for me to leg him up. He was laughing that much that eventually I got close enough to grab the furry hood of his Parker coat. We ended up in a heap in the snow and I spent ten minutes filling every pocket and opening on his clothing with snow. Down his back, front, his Parker hood, which was then pulled snuggly back on to his head to keep him nice and warm. I did notice after a while that his hysterical laughter had stopped, he was now pale blue and neither moving or breathing. Once we'd thawed him out and got his heart going again he seemed fine, so he was allowed to re-join his team to re-load.

To end the war of snow, our coup de grace was a real Dick Dastardly trick. We would form some smaller more compacted snowballs and leave them to harden. Then a lighter layer of a fluffy whiteness was added to help overcome accusations of attempted murder. A direct hit to the chest or skull with one of these beauties guaranteed an instant K.O. They would drop like they'd been hit by an assassin's bullet. Fortunately we knew how to place them in the recovery position. Once we'd fished their tongue out and slapped their cross eyed open mouthed gormless faces back to life, we would deny all knowledge of snowball tampering.

Richard swore blind we were loading them with rocks. We were doing no such thing. His sight returned later in the afternoon. It would be later in the day and going dark when we would go up to Ripon Road hill as a band of brothers and slide down on anything that guaranteed a near death experience. Just young lads having fun. Messing around and enjoying the snow. As John and I were older, we were allowed out a bit later. Half six, seven o'clock. We once walked up into town one evening, throwing snowballs at houses, lampposts, passing cars. Anything that made an easy target. It wasn't until we walked past The Regent Bingo Hall, that we realised we had stumbled upon a chance not to be missed. Queueing both outside and in the foyer itself were lots of elderly Bingo fanatics. We carried on walking for a while, and then made a quick arm full of lightly compacted fluff balls. Even we didn't want blacked out OAP's on our conscience. It was like shooting fish in a barrel. The screaming and cursing was X-rated, and from what I can remember, a tanned arse and a wrung neck were to be the preferred choices for our punishment. They would have to catch us first. The onslaught lasted a good five minutes. Some of the less feeble ones did load up, but slipped and fell over before getting a shot off. Some were actually laughing and enjoying it. Anything had to be more exciting than Bingo.

We had made a pact before we opened fire that we would not try and knock hats or heads off. At the height of our fast approaching victory, an annoyed little chap in an oversized maroon Bingo Hall jacket appeared. He would be best described as Ben Turpin or Hitler's smaller twin brother. He was enraged almost to the point of heart failure. He gave chase shouting and screaming what we could expect if he got his hands on us. He had no chance, we were like whippets, even at ten years old. We lured him well away from the hall before treating him to a pounding with snowballs too. We couldn't believe that he had yet another level of rage in his locker.

"If I catch you, you little bastards, I'll beat the holy living crap out of you!"

"Catch us?! Catch us?! You couldn't catch a dose pal!"

We had no idea what we meant, and were once again proved wrong about the levels of rage he possessed. We left cross eyed Ben's twin brother with his moustache twitching, covered in snow, screaming obscenities at the night sky in an otherwise silent and snow covered Blackpool Town Centre Street. John and I strolled home pleased with our night's work and got a bag of chips to celebrate. Lovely.

24. SIMPLE FISHERMEN

It was time to begin preparing for big school. Blackpool Grammar School. Me being a year older than my best buddy, meant I would be there in isolation for a year. I gave him full instructions to make sure he passed his eleven plus (by cheating). As a family, we would be on the move as well. I had spotted a house for sale in an avenue my Mum and Dad had always liked. A bit bigger semi with driveway, garage, and nearer to Stanley Park. It felt like we were moving to another continent; it was in fact, only five streets away. The end of an era though. The closing of a chapter of my life that when I look back now seems so wonderful, safe, happy, and idyllic. That's because it was. Lucky boy, David, lucky boy.

I could have filled thousands of pages with glimpses of a past that I will be eternally grateful for. Those instances and experiences have themselves become part of what the universe is, and always will be. Moments of passed time, that make up all that is and will ever be. How I wish I had kept a diary every day since the day I was able to write. Can you imagine the delight as you become older, revisiting the days of your childhood? How many of those memories that are stored away, are waiting to tell their tales again and again for the cast of characters who played their parts in real time. Photographs provide visual evidence of your moments in time. Written memories bring them bursting to life.

John and I had a healthy interest in fishing as young lads. My Mum and Dad, and John's Mum and Dad, Barrie and Brenda, knew only too well that we had fads that would only last five minutes. For this reason our early tackle ensembles would be cobbled together as gifts from other elderly relatives, who either no longer fished, or were dead. The rods we inherited looked like they had been unearthed in an ancient cave excavation. The reels were equally inept. We had no clue what we were doing which did nothing to improve our chances of catching anything. John caught my head once with a wild wayward cast. Thankfully, he put it back.

We bought fishing line of a strength that would have allowed us to reel in an angry Blue Whale. Our hooks were also so big that any fish in British waters passing by would believe it to be the anchor of a ship. This collection of comedy fishing expertise must have brought many a chuckle to the seasoned five rod pier huggers who were in the same sprawled out spot every day. Instead of authentic fishing tackle baskets, John and I were equipped with Adidas sports bags that contained better sandwiches and hot drinks than they did fish catching equipment. We were conned into buying more black-worm bait than we would require in a lifetime. Our enormous hooks had that much bait on them that they resembled lumpy black tennis balls. A half ounce weight was attached three feet from the hook, and the big moment had arrived. The first cast into the Irish sea from the jetty at the end of Blackpool North Pier.

The first attempt didn't go very far, due to the fact that the reel lock was still on. The hook and weight nearly swung back and took my face off. Fortunately all the other anglers were too busy looking at rod tips for signs of bites to notice a ten year old halfwit thrashing around behind them.

I can understand how some people might view fishing as a very boring waste of time and life. Most of these men on the pier preferred the savagery of the weather and the unwelcoming Irish Sea to their home lives.

Reel lock off, and final checks talked through with my equally unqualified pal, and we were ready for take-off. I decided on a run up for my second attempt. A few tottering steps towards the railings with my eye on the black lump and my finger on the line at the reel and, whoosh. I flung the eight-foot beach caster rod forward with all my might. The black lump was off and away on its long, long, journey to my fish supper dreams.

All was looking like a young angler's paradise, until the huge black mass of compacted dead worms hit the rusty brown Blackpool briny. The recoil from this mini nuclear impact came hurtling back up the line and terminated at my reel. It resulted in what's known in fishing circles as a great bird's nest. After the fifty foot drop down to the water, what seemed at first to be a world record breaking cast, was in fact, about twenty feet out from the bottom of the pier. My reel was engulfed with an impossible looking ball of tangled fishing line, rendering it jammed and useless. John was in hysterics as I tried to start and unpick the chaos. As it turned out, he had learnt very little from observing my dog's dinner of a first attempt. He diligently made all final checks before what he hoped would be a seamless demonstration of textbook casting. I kept glancing up to check on how he was doing. Ready, he took a few faltering steps towards the pier railings with his rod arched way back behind his head. Whoosh. He fired his rod towards the sea with a truly humongous effort (more like a ten year old Inspector Blakey from 'On the Buses'). His paternoster, with a number of hooks, weights, and enough food to feed all the fish in the sea for a decade, disappeared out across the coastal waters like a big beautiful metallic and congealed black worm UFO. His knowing nodding smile (that's right, a bit like Jesus did with me at Christmas) suggested that today, victory was his in the 'Don't make a great big prick of yourself on the pier' cup final.

I had to admit, leaving my fishing line train crash for a few moments, that it was indeed, a cast of truly legendary status. As I patted his back and admired the wonder of at least a fifty percent chance of our team now catching a fish, something dawned on us both at the same moment. John's reel was now completely empty of fishing line. We followed the gaze up the rod and to the tip. Having forgotten to secure one end of his line to the reel properly, John had just cast his banquet laden paternoster and two hundred yards of fishing line on a one-way journey to the bottom of the sea. When I could finally see again through my tears of uncontrolled laughter, I hauled my line back up by hand, happy that every crab for miles around had feasted like a king on black worm. John pretended to reel something back in from the sea. We dismantled all our excuses for fish catching equipment, packed it away, and went to get some chips to go with our packed sandwiches and flasks of hot milky coffee. We were fishermen of sorts, the simple kind.

Prior to our first attempt at sea fishing, we had decided to practice our angling abilities at Stanley Park Lake. A fresh water venue, where catching fish was so easy that even we managed to do so. It was like shooting fish in a barrel. Yes, very like pelting the weak and elderly with snowballs. A sign on the footpath by the lake clearly stated that the shooting of fish was prohibited. Armed to the teeth with sea fishing equipment, we stomped down to the Park with nothing but giddy expectation of a huge net full of record breaking specimen fish. It was April. There wasn't another single angler along the concreted area that was reserved for fishing. For very good reason. It was out of season. Lovely, we thought, we had the whole place to ourselves. We assembled our huge rods and tackled up with line, hooks and bait that was more in keeping for attracting Thresher Shark than Perch. We were, quite literally, clueless in sea tackle. Never let a complete lack of skill or knowledge stand in your way though. It was our mission statement and motto, it still is. Have a go, and if you make a complete and utter fool of yourself, no one will see because it's out of season. With our favourite half ounce weights and black worm aplenty, we were ready to pollute the Park Lake with our inept angling terrorism. After twenty minutes or so of thrashing around on the bank noisily, casting out, and reeling in, we were suddenly confronted by a Parky on his bike.

He appeared from nowhere. "What do you two clowns think you're doing?" was his kind and friendly introduction.

"Just fishing sir. Err yeah, err, yep, just fishing, why?"

"Why? Why?! I'll tell you why laddie, fishing season doesn't start for another month. You need a licence to fish, and you're using all the wrong tackle, that's why"

I did consider saying, "We're using all the right tackle, but not necessarily in the right location." but thought better of it on this occasion.

He was massive, and had a very severe short back and sides sticking out from under his Park Keeper's hat. His neck was also slightly wider than his head.

"Just pack up and clear off, and don't be so silly next time lads, alright? And make sure you get a ticket and use the right tackle okay?"

"Right sir, yes, sorry, will do, we didn't realise it was off season."

An hour later, he chased us of the grassed area where we were practicing casting towards the main road. He now had undeniable confirmation of our levels of clown stupidity. If he ever caught you riding your bike in the Park, you'd get a good clip round the ear. If there were Park Keepers now, God only knows what they would be faced with. Back then it was a cheeky response and run, or have him chase you on your bike to the little gap in the fence that he couldn't get through.

The very first fish that I caught was a modest sized dab off the pier. It was a moment of great pride and celebration. It was taken home with the intention of providing my family with a fish supper they would never forget. Mum assured me that there was only enough flesh on it to provide Tiddles, (the cat that urinated on me) with a tiny taste of the sea. However, we could capture the triumph on film as there were a few snaps left on the family camera. I stood jubilant in our back yard as Mum pointed and clicked at my outstretched arm and the record breaking specimen. A month or two later when we collected the fast track processing from Boots. There was a lovely picture of me smiling away at my angling success. Sadly though, the photo ended at my elbow, and instead of it being a picture of my fishing glory, it was merely a picture of me standing in the garden with my arm outstretched like an idiot.

All of Mum's photos ended up like this because she used to close the wrong eye when looking through the lens. Still, you got me in Mum. God bless you.

25. GREAT EXPECTATIONS

Now approaching the end of junior school and getting closer to the dreaded eleven plus ordeal, I would lie awake at night dreaming. I would dream I was fast asleep, dreaming that I was wide awake, thinking about things I could only dream about. When I finally fell asleep, I was awoken by a horrible dream that I was wide awake and couldn't fall asleep. I slept well as a child. What?! If you were expecting something more Dickensian, then you've come to the wrong shop. However, curiosity is a shop I do love to take a browse in from time to time. As indeed did Dickens. I think this chapter is going rather well so far, don't you? At least it all makes perfect sense.

This talk of dreaming was me lying awake worrying of course. Or as it's now known, being mentally ill. No, of course not, that would be crazy. That's what young boys do, right? Especially young boys who miraculously, by the power of lenient marking, have scraped through the trauma of their eleven plus, and have the chance of a much prized Grammar School education. That was my parents take on it, not mine. The pressure of what was expected of me was immense, even before the letter to confirm my choice of schools had arrived.

I remember the day well. I had just finished scrubbing the floor of my basement cell with sandpaper and bleach, when my Mum shouted for me to climb into the dumb waiter. I was then hoisted up into the forbidden living area. The smell of fresh air and the blinding daylight was most unsettling. Before I was allowed out of the securely barred transport cage I was placated with a banana or two to calm me down. They were delicious, and took away the taste of fish heads that were lowered down to me in a bucket twice a day. The bananas were such a treat that I barely noticed the icy blast of cold water from the power hose.

"Don't be silly David, that didn't happen, stop being daft"

"Oh, hi Mum." Alright, alright, I was shouted down from my lovely comfortable bedroom where I had my nose buried in some fascinating educational textbook. The one I had sneaked in, entitled 'How to wing it at Grammar School'.

My nose was buried in it, because I had slumped forward fast asleep, and was dreaming about scrubbing my cell floor with bleach.

"David! It's here, the letter about your choice of school has arrived."

I felt sick. I knew my Mum and Dad were really hoping that I had passed. We wouldn't have been able to live with the shame and ridicule had I not got through. Their words, not mine. My sister Kate was already doing well at the girls' Collegiate School, so the honour of the family name was at stake. Mmm... steak. I had butterflies in my stomach as I scampered downstairs to finally find out my fate. It was either bananas or butterflies, I can't remember now.

The rest of the family were gathered around the dining room table nervously looking at the brown envelope and its little opaque window. Their nerves were wholly justified. I had just remembered a moment when reading aloud at Junior School where I pronounced 'facsimile' as 'fascist smile'. An easy mistake to make when you're seven years old and nervous. I smiled weakly, (sometimes daily) as I picked up the envelope to put us all out of our misery. Me especially. With a flourish of fake excitement, I tore into the details of my future like a demented daydreamer doing his best to appear interested. I held the sheet aloft and frantically scanned the squiggles on the page in blind panic. That didn't help at all, so I instructed my eyeballs to stop acting daft and read the bloody thing. There in glorious black and white was the choice that my parents had laid awake at night dreaming about.

Arnold, St. Josephs, Hodgson, Blackpool Grammar School. Joyous cheers, hair ruffling and back slapping all round.

"That's fantastic son (they forgot my name sometimes), we told you you weren't a complete idiot."

"That's lovely David, well done sunny Jim." was my Mum's proud smiling boast (Mum got my name right at least 80% of the time). Not like my Gran. She would run through the names of every other living relative on the planet before finally arriving at David. It was usually because she was in a rage at me for doing something stupid or cheeky. Or both.

"Are you excited?" Mum asked with encouraging enthusiasm.

"Well I feel sick if that's any help?"

"Well that's because you're excited that's all."

I wasn't convinced. My Dad then made matters much worse. After a pretence bunch of fives to my chin, and a knowing well done son wink, he kindly informed me that this was when the hard work really begins. Cheers Dad, I feel even more like barfing now.

I decided at this point not to ask if acting the goat and day dreaming would be enough to ensure a hat full of qualifications. It wasn't. Hogarth, you're an idiot. Cheers, thanks very much. Their faces were so happy and proud that I couldn't bring myself to ruin the moment with a trademark stupid comment. Instead my Mum started to make plans immediately to ring every other living soul she knew with the barely believable news that bird brain was off to Grammar School. She also began to plan a shopping trip into town to equip me with all the ridiculous items of uniform we were required to wear.

Two other things sank in at this point. It was an all-boys' school, which while it was good for concentration in class, it did nothing for my favourite pastime of day dreaming about girls. Secondly, they didn't play football, only rugby. Even worse, it was rugby union. My Dad did his best as a rugby hating liar to convince me that rugby wasn't all that bad, and I could at least take the kick offs and conversions if needs be. What about the other seventy eight minutes standing around freezing my nuts off and avoiding being crushed to death by abnormally large men pretending to be eleven year old boys?

"Just dribble around them, and boot it up the other end of the pitch." was my Father's life saving advice! In fairness, for the most part, it worked.

With only a few stomach churning weeks left before the start of term, Mum was keen to get me into town and kitted out. As my Dad had a decent job, it meant every damn thing on the list was going to be purchased. My sulky persona on the trip only prompted her to keep reminding me how proud I should be of such an opportunity.

"Yeah, but they don't even play footy for God's sake."

"Oh David, stop being so silly will you? You can play football when you get home from school, and on the park at weekends with your mates. You're football daft, just be grateful you've got in at Grammar School. There are loads of kids that would jump at a chance like that."

"Yeah, I suppose."

Damn clever these Mums you know? I'd never thought about it like that. Besides, you've missed something Mum. I'm not football daft, I'm just daft. Later to advance to bonkers, all being well. I certainly had the credentials for it. A day dreaming halfwit with a terrifying imagination who disliked anyone who appeared to have no personality or sense of humour. That's right, adults.

Well, that may be a tad unfair, I did like Tommy Cooper, Morecambe and Wise, Laurel and Hardy and my Mum and Dad. In fact, my Mum and Dad were funnier than most of the comedians of the era, despite being blissfully unaware of it. My Gran was even funnier still. One of her most used catchphrases when tittle tattling about other female neighbours was,

"Horrible woman."

This label of unwavering certainty could be applied for something as innocuous as the condition of their front step, or, a particular shade of cardigan they happened to be wearing.

"Navy blue?! In July!?… horrible woman."

She was lucky she wasn't a chimpanzee (the woman in navy blue, not my Gran). Her second favourite and more scathing comment reserved for primates was,

"Filthy creatures."

This would be barked out at the very appearance of a monkey, cheeky or otherwise. She would actually cover the TV screen with a newspaper if one was ever bold enough to make an appearance.

Yes, it's true to say, there was only one thing that my Gran hated… everything! (Especially neighbours and monkeys) In fairness, some were one and the same thing. I have often wondered where my sometimes prickly nature originated from. How she failed to notice my resemblance to the chimp branch of evolution is a mystery. Having said that, she very rarely got my name right, ever.

Anyway, back to the shopping trip. There were two 'official' stockists of school attire in Blackpool. Oh yes, this was serious stuff. The black market in counterfeit school uniforms was a huge problem in Blackpool in the seventies. You couldn't walk through town without some dodgy geezer approaching you and asking,

"Need a grammar school tie or rugby shirt, fella?"

It was horrible, and intimidating. The competition for trade was ferocious. Orry's and Rawcliffe's outfitters were only some hundred yards apart on Church Street. They knew every trick in the book. Adverts in the Gazette, posters on bus stop shelters, imaginative window displays featuring provocative child mannequins in saucy 'back to school' poses. You didn't stand a chance. Some of the poses were less than credulous to be perfectly honest. Why would you have one hand shielding your eyes and forehead as if saluting, while your other arm appeared to be pointing to a ship somewhere out at sea? The girl dummy in this grotesque pastiche, would be partially bent over, cross legged, and her index finger pressed alluringly into her cheek (facial cheek!). God only knows what was going through the window dresser's mind? Or mine, come to that.

Mum split the uniform list between the two shops. There was a leaning towards Rawcliffe's, although that could have been the force seven gale coming up Church Street off the Irish Sea. Nothing to do with the small levels of schoolboy flatulence coming from my trousers. Orry's was a bit swankier in the pricing of items. It was a lovely shop. Long gone now as Blackpool town centre continues to lose a great deal of its old charm. We would get the dearer items at Rawcliffe's which were cheaper there, and the cheaper items at Orry's which were dearer than the identical items at Rawcliffe's. Orry's was a much trendier place with, let's just say, flamboyant male members of staff, who had more than an eye for any discerning follower of fashion. I'm sure they used to measure my inside leg.

"Get your thumb out of my gonads Mister, or I'll stick the nut on you."

I would think to myself as the guy checked for the fifth time that he'd got it right. My Mum would watch on, smiling and insisting,

"Hold still now, while this nice young man feels you up a bit."

"Don't be silly David, that didn't happen. Where you get all this nonsense from is beyond me. You've got way too much of a vivid imagination young man."

Correct Mum (as always). Besides, you would have nutted him yourself.

Don't worry though Mum, it's only me making stuff up and acting daft as usual. I'm off to Grammar School in a few weeks. They'll soon put that little bonfire out. To this day, I still know nothing about anything. I prefer it that way. It leaves more room for thinking.

"Well that's all very well young man, but you still need some school shoes and a satchel."

A satchel!? A satchel!? Have you gone mad woman? (I would think). Do you want me to get duffed up on my first day at school?

"Don't pull a face David, it's on the list. You can't use your football kit bag, it's not allowed, and besides, all the other boys will have them."

The selection of said satchels, was more, sad satchels. My expression when presented with them to make a choice resembled that of a wide eyed confused frightened rabbit, who was about to vomit.

"Oh for goodness sake David, pick one, and be quick about it."

With my mouth open, and dry with disbelief, I stretched out a trembling arm, and ashamedly pointed at the one I hated the least.

"Finally, thank you, we'll take that one thanks."

The flamboyant male shop assistant gave my Mum a sympathetic pained smile. He gave me a discreet bitchy glare for my obvious disgust at his hideous range of high quality school book containers. I was then dragged into the shoe department, with bitchy glare in tow, to get the final piece of the jigsaw, school shoes.

I had managed to convince Mum that the trendy all the rage 'Wayfinders' would be the hard wearing sensible option. They were ingeniously equipped with animal print soles and a compass secreted inside the heel. They were a key bit of Cub Scout footwear. It did come to my notice that the prints belonged largely to animals not native to British shores. Also, the compass was so tiny that you needed a magnifying glass to locate and read it. There was no secret compartment for a magnifying glass, so all in all, a complete waste of time. They had a strong marketing team at 'Wayfinders' though, and that was good enough for any bonkers eleven year old kid who was in the scouts.

I was now fully kitted out and ready to, if required, identify the hoof print of a Hippopotamus, and then, whilst peering through a magnifying glass into my shoe, hop towards the North Pole, in Blackpool.

My best pal John, on hearing of my shoe acquisition,

pestered his Mum into submission for a pair. Oh yes, we spent many an hour hopping around Stanley Park's muddied areas comparing the soles of our shoes to imprints in the soil. Our holy grail was the paw print of a badger. There were no badgers in Stanley Park. This did not deter us. It was the only near achievable animal print that we would ever have a chance of finding. After hours of hopping and hoping, we finally convinced ourselves that the paw print of a Golden Retriever was that of a larger than average badger. Exhausted from breaking the world hopping record, we made our way West North West to the park gates, and home for tea. Were it not for the miniature compasses, we might have never made it home at all... ever.

When the first day of secondary school finally arrived, I reluctantly boarded the school special along with my stupid satchel, and stupid cap. I knew they were stupid, as they belonged to me. The next five years was an anxiety filled mish-mash of emotions, and in all honesty, a complete blur. I do remember throwing my cap out of the bus window on the way home on day one however. The first two years went okay, then the girl's collegiate school joined up with us, and bang went my education. My first girlfriend encounter at about age thirteen introduced me to the delights of having a female stick her tongue in your mouth to enhance the experience of kissing. It came as a mind blowing shock that this was indeed what was supposed to happen. I rather naively assumed that you just stuck closed lips together and made moaning noises to indicate your enjoyment. I was about to pull back in disgusted bewilderment, when I suddenly received a message from the underpants department encouraging me to give it a few more seconds. I had a quick five minutes more of tongue fencing with my newly acquired and very tasty best friend, before telling her I had to dash off as U.F.O. was on at six o'clock. My first proper snog had been successfully accomplished only to be relegated in the pecking order below a Gerry Anderson inspired T.V. show. Those damned aliens have got a lot to answer for.

26. TWO FAST ONES, PLEASE

Before we have a final quick ride on the donkeys at the beach and head home, here are some of the key tunes that I have a seemingly infinite connection to from those precious early memories. When you wish upon a Star- (Jiminy Cricket) Pinocchio. I wanna be like you- (King Louis) Jungle Book. If I were a rich man- (Topol) Fiddler on the Roof. Blue ridged mountains of Virginia- Laurel and Hardy. I'm a believer- Alternate Title- The Monkees. Penny Lane- Lady Madonna- Get Back-The Beatles. Mony Mony- Tommy James and The Shondells. Young girl- Union Gap. Eloise-Barry Ryan. Dance to the music-Sly and the family Stone. Fire Brigade- Blackberry Way-The Move. Light my Fire- Jose Feliciano. Do it again- The Beach boys. Sugar Sugar- The Archies. The Israelites-Desmond Decker. First of May- Bee Gees. The Upsetters-Return of Django. Stevie Wonder- My Cherie Amour- For once in my life. Space Oddity- David Bowie.

A soundtrack for a five to ten year old young lad, who was next to enter the terrifying world of serious education. Secondary school. How I scraped through my eleven plus is a miracle. Possibly thanks to Mrs. Crawford's pep talk regarding me pulling my damn socks up and not daydreaming and acting daft all the time.

During the summer months, John and I would be permanently down on the prom or the beach looking at scantily clad grockles making fools of themselves. Trousers rolled up, hankies on heads, third degree burns. There were always lots and lots of girlie grockles too. Not that we were capable of anything other than gawping at them and then having an early night. It was just great to be down on the beach, mucking about with a ball, or catching crabs from around the pier legs. The first donkey ride we had, was a rite of passage. It was a chance to prove as a young virile male, that you could ride a wild steed (an ancient Donkey) for miles at top speed (two hundred yards at a little above walking pace).

Your first request to the fat bald man with more gaps than teeth in a vest was, 'Two fast ones please'. If you were there with your mate, of course. The chances of any of these beasts of burden being capable of fast, was remote. They stood there looking uninterested or asleep. Once two had been selected by the wily donkey mogul, you would be given the complex instructions regarding staying alive during the experience.

"Keep your feet in the stirrups and hold on to the handle."

Now that you were much closer to these animals, they seemed a lot bigger than you imagined. A lot smellier too. Ethel and Rocket were singled out for duty. I climbed on Rocket quickly before John spotted the names. I smiled, and nodded knowingly as he finally realised he was getting on a donkey called Ethel. We were clad in T-shirts, swimming trunks, and plastic sandals. The sandals were more painful to wear than the hard ridged sand or the sting of a jellyfish could ever be. Once the donkeys were readied and facing the right way, the CEO of the company would verbally abuse them with words like, "Gertcha." You were then subjected to a terrifying ordeal that seemed to last forever.

Trying desperately to remain in the saddle and look cool, your body was shaken to pieces during the two minute sprint. At times, hurling yourself to the safety of the hard wet sand seemed like a sensible option, but you clung on and allowed the pounding saddle to mash your newly forming testicles into a paste. You would then alight after the unpleasant experience and lie and boast about how fantastic it was.

"Another run lads?" the donkey herder asked.

Err no, you're okay mate, me nuts have been irreparably damaged on the first run thanks. We would spend the rest of the afternoon walking around bow legged and fretting about what untold damage had been done to our crushed crown jewels.

As a full complement of donkeys went zooming past on a busy run one afternoon in July, the shrieks and screams of a child jockey were plainly audible. A saddle had slipped round and the unfortunate infant was now under the stampeding beast having to endure a whole new version of a donkey ride. Thankfully the donkey was uninjured. Two free rides on a fast one with tight straps was the extent of the compensation package for the kid.

My first real challenge in life, other than remaining in the saddle of a stampeding donkey, was to pass my eleven plus. Pressure from my Dad, not so much my Mum. I had scraped through my first character challenge and made it to an all-boys Grammar School. I'm not sure my Dad was confident for much more. He tried his best to drive it home that now was when the hard work really did begin. It was a hand on shoulder Father and Son moment that was supposed to get me not to make a hash of the next five years. Whoops!

"Dad? When I grow up, am I going to be a failure?"

"Yes son … a spectacular failure."

They didn't even play football at Grammar School. I considered blowing my eleven plus based on that very fact.

There would be two years of boys only freedom before the girl's joined up. Goodbye Emma Peel, goodbye education. Hello young ladies, ridiculous fashions, bad haircuts, kissing, dancing, drinking, and tons of other toe curling embarrassments.

Life though, I suppose, is a little bit like being sent in to bat at cricket. You arrive at the crease nervous, but you are kitted out with all that you need to survive and do well. You have a good look around to explore your options and take guard in preparation. Then you have to stand there and take whatever life throws at you. You don't really know what's coming next, but somehow you keep fending off ball after ball and surviving. You have to play all the tough deliveries really carefully and with a straight defensive bat. When you get the odd loose ball, you whack it out of the park. Sometimes you swing and miss, other times you miss completely and take a few painful blows. Hopefully you have remembered a box for scrotal protection. Keep batting as long as you can, and enjoy your innings while it lasts. Carry a big heavy bat and never let life terrify you into being bowled out first ball for a duck. Even if you get 1, then that is better than 0, right? Something... or nothing... you choose.

My Mum bought me my first proper cricket bat, I made quite a few runs with it too. I get the feeling she's still batting with me on my side every day. It's nice to have your Mum in your heart when you walk out to bat.

When she passed away, I thought she was gone forever. I was sinking and falling apart at the seams. I now know that she is with me always, forever. How could I possibly ever doubt my curtains and the newspaper crossword clues that I see with my own eyes.

Now, where's my bat, pads and notebook? Yes, where

is your notebook? Hogarth… you're an idiot. Well, what do you expect from a daydreaming halfwit who cost sixpence from a stall at Fleetwood Market?

Thanks for reading this, Mum, and for you and Dad helping me to write it too. I don't think I could have managed without you as my guiding light. Keep it shining bright won't you? It will help me to find my way home.

We are all here alone, together. The tips of threads that stretch back to the very beginning of time. 13.8 billion years from home. Raise your eyes to the heavens, smile at the stars, and let the Universe see your face. It knows exactly who you are… so does your Mum.

the end – so far

mum and me, 1985

ACKNOWLEDGEMENTS

Louise Dean, founder, author, and owner at the creative writing site, 'The Novelry', for all your patience, belief, and expertise.

John Parker, and the Parker family, great friends, and wonderful memories from our early years' adventures.

Kathryn Holman, psychic and spiritual guide, for being a friend and great listener.

Peter and Cheryl Wolstencroft, for your kindness and unwavering support.

To all other friends and relatives, past and present, for your support, guidance and encouragement.

To my publishers for their direction and advice.

Finally, to all the characters who have featured in my own personal history. 'God bless us, everyone.'

Colour Your Reading

8 to 12:	Green
YA:	Red
Adult:	Magenta
Poetry:	Blue
Non-Fiction:	Gold

Hawkwood Books 2024